NAME

SHARPEN YOUR SKILLS

Using a Problem-Solving Guide

How many 3-digit numbers greater than 700 are there in which the sum of the digits is 16? Exercises 1–4 will help you solve this problem.

1. Give 3 examples of numbers that fit the conditions.

2. Can such a number include the digit 1 and the digit 3? Why or why not?

3. Give all such numbers with 9 hundreds and 6 tens. Do the same for 9 hundreds and 5 tens.

4. Give all such numbers greater than 900.

5. Continue the method used in Exercises 3 and 4 to find how many 3-digit numbers greater than 700 there are in which the sum of the digits is 16.

Solve each problem. **Remember** to refer to the problem-solving guide for help and tips.

6. How many digits are written to list the numbers from 0–50?

7. How many digits in Exercise 6 are 5s?

8. Write the largest number and the smallest number you can using all the digits from 1–9 exactly once in each. Subtract the smaller from the larger. What is the difference?

NAME

SHARPEN YOUR SKILLS

Sequences

Tell whether the sequence is arithmetic, geometric, or neither. Then write the next three terms.

1. $2^2, 2^4, 2^8 \ldots$

2. 1, 10, 100, 1,000, 10,000, . . .

3. 18, 20, 22, 24, . . .

4. 5, 10, 15, 20, 25, . . .

5. 0, 2, 3, 5, 6, . . .

6. 1, 5, 9, 13, 17, . . .

7. 4, 8, 16, 32, 64, . . .

8. 10, 30, 50, . . .

9. $1, 1\frac{1}{2}, 2, 2\frac{1}{2}, \ldots$

10. 0.4, 0.04, 0.004, . . .

11. $\frac{1}{4}, 1, 4, 16, 64, \ldots$

12. 13, 19, 25, 31, . . .

Find the missing terms.

13. 3, ____ , ____ , 12, 15

14. 0.2, 0.04, ____ , ____ , 0.00032

15. ____ , 9, 27, ____ , 243

16. $\frac{1}{4}, \frac{1}{8},$ ____ , ____ , $\frac{1}{64}$

NAME ______

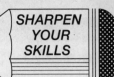

SHARPEN YOUR SKILLS

Fibonacci Sequence

Use these numbers of the Fibonacci sequence to answer the questions.

Fibonacci Sequence 1, 1, 2, 3, 5, 8, 13, 21, 34, 55, . . .

1. How are the numbers in the Fibonacci sequence related? What is the rule?

______

2. Which positions in the sequence are occupied by even numbers? ______

3. Which positions are multiples of 5? ______

4. Which positions in the sequence are multiples of 4? ______

Use the same rule used to construct the Fibonacci sequence to construct each of these sequences. Tell whether you used mental math or paper and pencil.

5. 2, 5, 7, 12, ☐, ☐, ☐, . . . ______

6. 4, 9, 13, 22, ☐, ☐, ☐, . . . ______

7. 3, ☐, 12, ☐, 33, ☐, . . . ______

Critical Thinking Solve the problems about the Fibonacci sequence.

8. Two successive Fibonacci numbers are 75,025 and 121,393. Find the number that came before.

______

9. Two successive Fibonacci numbers are 28,657 and 46,368. Find the two numbers that came before.

______

NAME

SHARPEN YOUR SKILLS

Pascal's Triangle

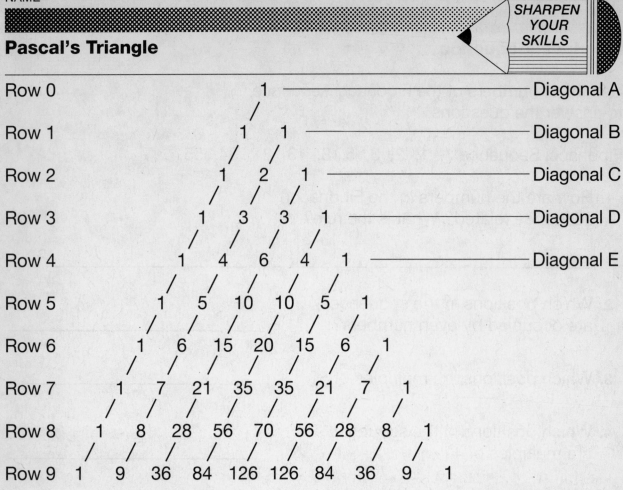

Row 0	1	Diagonal A
Row 1	1 1	Diagonal B
Row 2	1 2 1	Diagonal C
Row 3	1 3 3 1	Diagonal D
Row 4	1 4 6 4 1	Diagonal E
Row 5	1 5 10 10 5 1	
Row 6	1 6 15 20 15 6 1	
Row 7	1 7 21 35 35 21 7 1	
Row 8	1 8 28 56 70 56 28 8 1	
Row 9	1 9 36 84 126 126 84 36 9 1	

Use Pascal's triangle to answer the questions.
Remember that row 0 is the first row of the triangle.

1. What pattern do you see in row 9?

____

____

____

2. What numbers will be in row 12?

____

____

____

3. What will the second number in row 44 be?

____

4. Which numbers in row 7 are divisible by 7?

____

Critical Thinking Solve these problems about Pascal's triangle.

5. In which diagonal would you find these three numbers: 45, 55, 66?

____

6. In which diagonal would you find these three numbers: 120, 165, 220?

____

NAME

SHARPEN YOUR SKILLS

Solve a Simpler Problem

Solve each problem.

1. What is the sum of the first 4 odd numbers? the first 5? the first 500?

2. Stacey has 7 blouses and 6 skirts. How many different blouse-skirt combinations are possible?

3. There are 12 teams in a basketball league. In a tournament, each team will play each of the other teams once. How many games will be played?

4. John has 8 pairs of slacks, 10 shirts, and 4 sweaters. From how many different combinations can he choose if he chooses slacks, a shirt, and a sweater each time?

5. The eighth-grade class has 16 girls and 14 boys. How many different one boy-one girl committees can be arranged?

6. If a coin is tossed 5 times, in how many different ways can the sequence of heads and tails appear?

7. How many two-person committees can be formed from a group of six people?

8. There are 7 books on a library shelf. Three are math books and 4 are literature books. In how many different ways can the books be arranged so all math books are together?

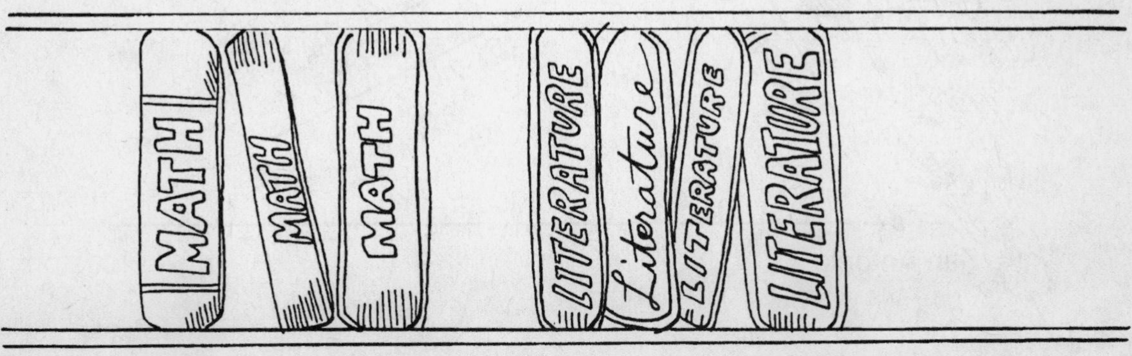

NAME

SHARPEN YOUR SKILLS

Estimation Strategies

Estimate each answer.

1. 835 + 629 + 186 ____________
2. 325 × 489 ____________
3. 8,647 ÷ 48 ____________
4. 1,856 − 745 ____________
5. $3.65 + 4.19 + 3.95 ____________
6. $15.95 ÷ $.37 ____________
7. 85 × 42 ____________
8. $28\overline{)945}$ ____________
9. 435 + 267 + 119 ____________
10. 325 + 275 + 309 ____________

In Exercises 11 and 12, use the diagram to estimate each answer.

11. Jane travels from San Antonio to Austin and back twice a week. About how many miles does she travel each week? About how many miles does she travel in a month?

____

12. Sam travels from Houston to Austin and then to San Antonio on business four times a week. He returns directly from San Antonio to Houston. About how far does he travel in a week?

____

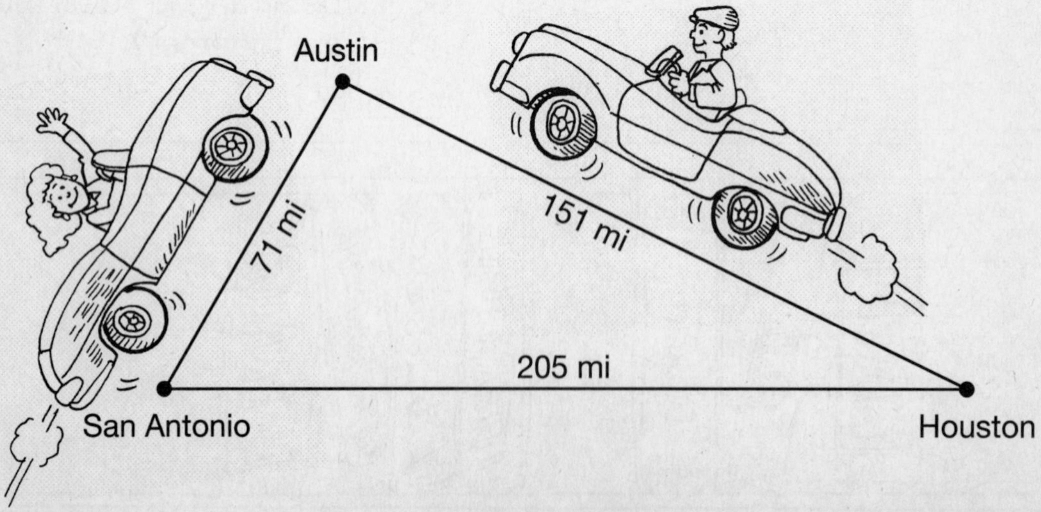

NAME

Evaluating Expressions

SHARPEN YOUR SKILLS

Number the steps to solve the problem using the standard order of operations.

1. $\frac{45 + 4 \times 3}{12}$

____ add 45

____ multiply 4×3

____ divide by 12

2. $\frac{(36 + 3) \div (4 + 9)}{6}$

____ $36 + 3$; $4 + 9$

____ divide by 6

____ $39 \div 13$

Compute using the standard order of operations.

3. $14 + 2 - 3$ ____

4. $(21 - 17) + 4$ ____

5. $24(12 - 8)$ ____

6. $6(18 - 6) + 12$ ____

7. $(14 + 25) \div (9 - 4)$ ____

8. $\frac{95 - 90 + 6 \times 2}{11}$ ____

9. $\frac{4(3 - 3)}{6(5 + 4)}$ ____

10. $\frac{(14 + 6)}{2(3 + 2)}$ ____

Evaluate each expression when $x = 10$ and $y = 5$.

11. $2x - 3y$ ____

12. $2y(x - 3)$ ____

13. $\frac{2}{x} + \frac{3}{y}$ ____

14. $2(x + y)$ ____

15. $\frac{2x + y}{3}$ ____

16. $x + y - (x - y)$ ____

Place parentheses to make the statement true.

17. $18 + 2 - 3 + 6 = 11$

18. $4 \times 3 + 6 = 36$

19. $6 \times 12 + 4 + 4 = 100$

Insert the correct computation sign between the numbers so that the statement is true.

20. 4 ____ 6 ____ 8 ____ 2 = 1

NAME

SHARPEN YOUR SKILLS

Interpret the Remainder

Solve each problem. Decide how the remainder should be used.

1. In the Chez Ritz restaurant, 6 people can sit at each table. How many tables are needed to seat 34 people?

   ____

   How many people will sit at the last table?

   ____

2. Cary, a waiter at the Chez Ritz, earned $53 in tips in 5 hours. How much did he average per hour?

   ____

3. The chef at the Chez Ritz uses an average of 42 pounds of round steak per day. Ground round steak is sold in 5-pound packages. How many packages must be purchased per day?

   ____

4. The owner of the Chez Ritz plans to have new tablecloths made for the restaurant. If each tablecloth takes 6 yards of material, how many tablecloths can be made from 275 yards of material?

   ____

   How much material will be left?

   ____

5. If each waiter at the Chez Ritz serves 5 tables, how many waiters are needed to serve 43 tables?

   ____

   Will all waiters have 5 tables to serve?

   ____

6. Napkins come in packages of 35. If the owner of Chez Ritz wants to order 500 napkins, how many packages must he order?

   ____

7. On a Saturday night, the Chez Ritz took in a total of $2,486 on 31 checks. What was the average amount spent per check?

   ____

NAME

SHARPEN YOUR SKILLS

Mental Math Strategies

Use mental math to do each computation.

1. 84 − 36

2. 237 + 245

3. 7 × 54

4. 68 + 72

5. 4,002 − 385

6. 1,523 × 8

7. 27 + 33 + 42 + 18

8. 15 × 64

9. 148 + 35 + 23

10 28 + 364

11. 13 × 48

12. 12 × 38

13. 45 + 86 + 79

14. 223 + 487

15. 147 × 500

16. 220 + 830 + 610

17. 24 + 35 + 26

18. 27 × 999

19. Give a method for multiplying by 20 using mental math.

20. Give a method for multiplying by 50 using mental math.

NAME

SHARPEN YOUR SKILLS

Choose a Computation Method

Use mental math, paper and pencil, or calculator to find the answer. Tell which method you used.

1. $25 \times 8{,}640$

2. $(365 + 426) - 210$

3. $82{,}365 - 26{,}192$

4. 700×23

5. 450×0.001

6. $0.26325 \div 0.05$

Solve each problem. Tell whether you used mental math, paper and pencil, or calculator.

7. James went on a 450 mile bicycle trip. He was on his bicycle for 90 hours total. How many miles did he average per hour?

8. Rob spent 85 hours on his homework the first month of school. The second month of school he spent 65 hours on his homework. If he spent $\frac{1}{5}$ of each month's time on math, what was his total time spent on math?

Estimation Estimate each answer. Tell which estimation strategy you used.

9. 33,175–11,746

10. $50 \times 62{,}345$

Use after pages 26–27.

NAME

SHARPEN YOUR SKILLS

Factors and Divisibility

Find all the factors of the given number. Tell whether the number is prime or composite. **Remember** to use the divisibility rules.

1. 60

2. 45

3. 17

4. 51

5. 121

6. 75

7. 61

8. 39

Find each answer.

9. Give the first 5 multiples of 12.

10. Are any multiples of 2 prime numbers?

11. Of three numbers, two are prime. The sum of the three is a multiple of 8, and their product is 126. What are the numbers?

Mental Math Give the first ten multiples of 9. Can you give all of the multiples of 9? Explain your answer.

NAME

SHARPEN YOUR SKILLS

Exponents and Prime Factorization

Write the prime factorization of each number in exponential form. **Remember** to include all the factors in your answer.

1. 64

2. 150

3. 225

4. 60

5. 24

6. 3,000

7. 12,600

8. 480

9. 1,650

Express each product as a power of 5.

10. $5^3 \times 5^2$

11. $5^4 \times 5^0$

12. $5^{12} \times 5^6 \times 5^3$

13. $5^{23} \times 5^4$

14. $5^{100} \times 5^2 \times 5^3$

15. $5^2 \times 5^4 \times 5^6 \times 5^{14}$

Critical Thinking Solve each problem.

16. Write $3^5 \times 9^2$ as a power of 3.

17. Write $4^4 \times 16^2$ as a power of 2.

18. How many ways can you write 5^4 as the product of two factors?

NAME

SHARPEN YOUR SKILLS

Common Factors and Equal Fractions

Find the GCF for the given numbers.
Remember to find all the common factors.

1. 36, 72 ________

2. 75, 45 ________

3. 56, 72 ________

4. 68, 119 ________

5. 36, 60 ________

6. 48, 112 ________

7. 14, 18, 22 ________

8. 54, 126 ________

9. 49, 64 ________

10. 60, 80, 120 ________

11. 32, 64, 80 ________

12. 27, 81, 135 ________

Write each fraction in lowest terms.

13. $\frac{42}{63}$ ________

14. $\frac{18}{72}$ ________

15. $\frac{35}{60}$ ________

16. $\frac{21}{56}$ ________

17. $\frac{24}{84}$ ________

18. $\frac{150}{450}$ ________

19. $\frac{270}{600}$ ________

20. $\frac{49}{130}$ ________

Critical Thinking Find each answer.

21. If two numbers are prime, their GCF is 1. What is true about the LCM of the numbers?

____

22. What is the relationship between the LCM and GCF of two numbers?

____

____

____

NAME

SHARPEN YOUR SKILLS

Common Multiples and Common Denominators

Find the LCM for the given numbers.

1. 24, 16 ________

2. 40, 50 ________

3. 5, 8, 12 ________

4. 2, 9, 12 ________

5. 25, 40 ________

6. 6, 14, 20 ________

7. 8, 12, 16 ________

8. 5, 12, 20 ________

9. 24, 36 ________

10. 12, 10 ________

11. 20, 25 ________

12. 8, 9, 12 ________

Tell which fraction is larger.

13. $\frac{5}{8}$ $\frac{1}{3}$ ________

14. $\frac{5}{6}$ $\frac{8}{24}$ ________

15. $\frac{1}{7}$, $\frac{1}{4}$, $\frac{1}{2}$, ________

16. $\frac{7}{10}$, $\frac{2}{3}$, $\frac{4}{5}$, ________

17. $\frac{5}{6}$, $\frac{3}{4}$, $\frac{7}{8}$, ________

18. $\frac{7}{8}$ $\frac{4}{5}$ ________

Write the fractions in order from smallest to largest.

19. $\frac{4}{9}$ $\frac{3}{4}$ $\frac{5}{6}$ ________

20. $\frac{7}{8}$ $\frac{9}{10}$ $\frac{5}{6}$ ________

Mixed Practice Find the LCM and the GCF for each group of numbers.

21. 18, 24 ________

22. 12, 48 ________

23. 20, 10, 15 ________

24. 3, 5, 9 ________

NAME

SHARPEN YOUR SKILLS

Dividing a Decimal by a Whole Number

Divide the number in the center by each of the numbers around it. Use a calculator when needed.

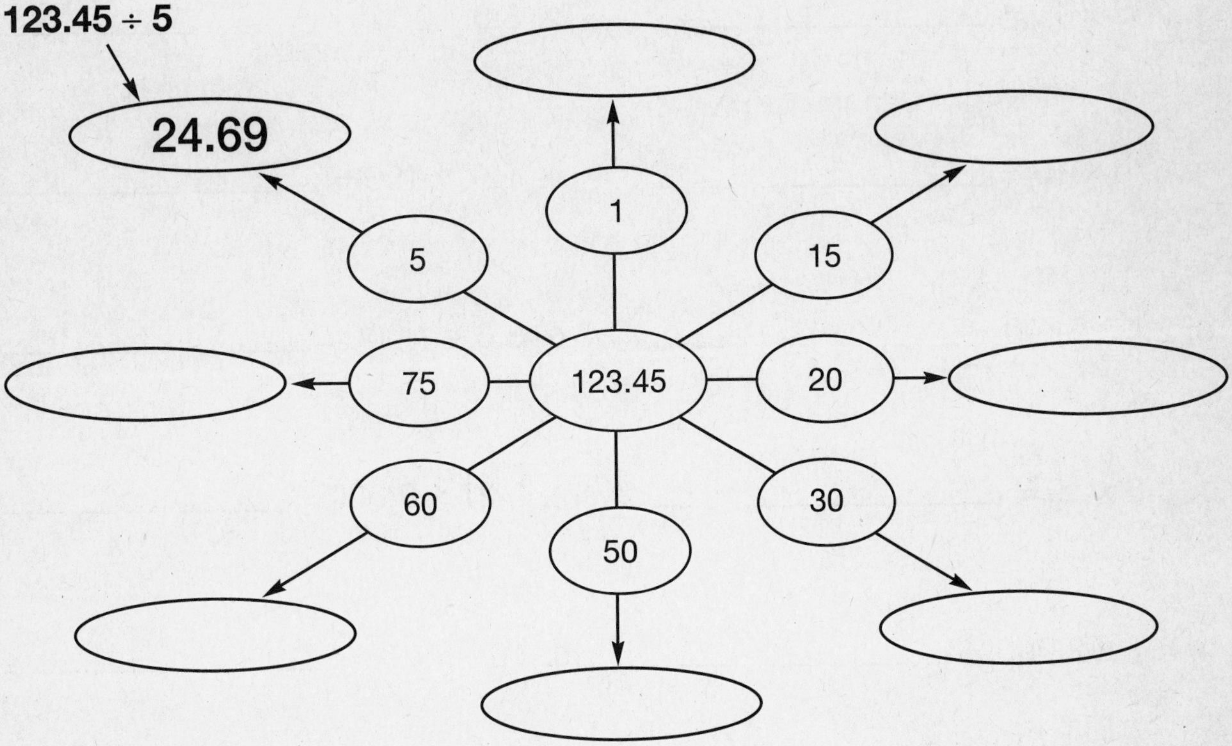

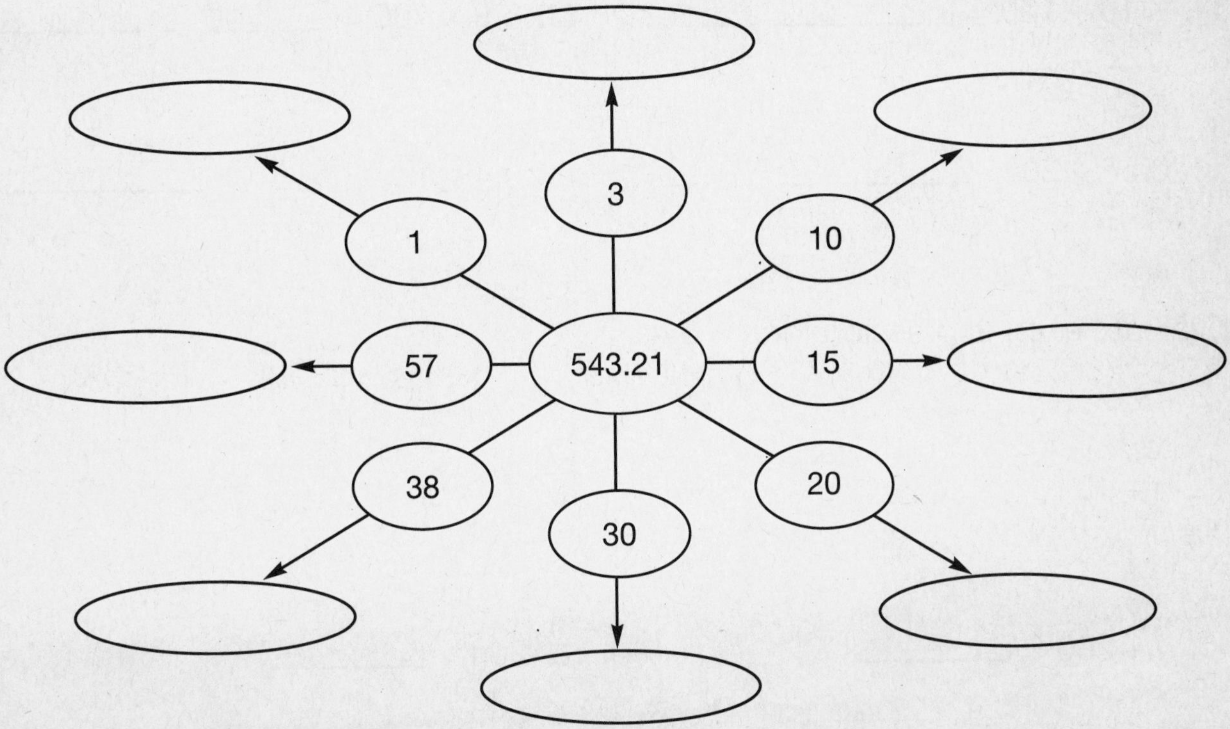

Use after pages 48-49.

NAME

Multiplying and Dividing by Multiples of 10

SHARPEN YOUR SKILLS

Tell whether you would use mental math or paper and pencil. Then compute.

1. $235 \times 10 =$ ____________

2. $8.6 \div 200 =$ ____________

3. $679 \times 10 =$ ____________

4. $127 \times 100 =$ ____________

5. $2.47 \div 100 =$ ____________

6. $8.6 \div 1{,}000 =$ ____________

7. $3.6 \times 20 =$ ____________

8. $0.27 \times 3{,}000 =$ ____________

9. $6.7 \times 2{,}000 =$ ____________

10. $16 \div 10 =$ ____________

11. $7.15 \div 100 =$ ____________

12. $9.9 \times 100 =$ ____________

13. $0.56 \div 20 =$ ____________

14. $0.4 \div 100 =$ ____________

Evaluate each expression for $n = 3.4$.

15. $n \div 10 =$ ________

16. $n \div 100 =$ ________

17. $n \div 200 =$ ________

18. $20n =$ ________

NAME

Dividing a Decimal by a Decimal

SHARPEN YOUR SKILLS

Why doesn't the ocean overflow the land?

To find out, divide. Find each answer at the right. Write the letter for that exercise. Two answers are not used.

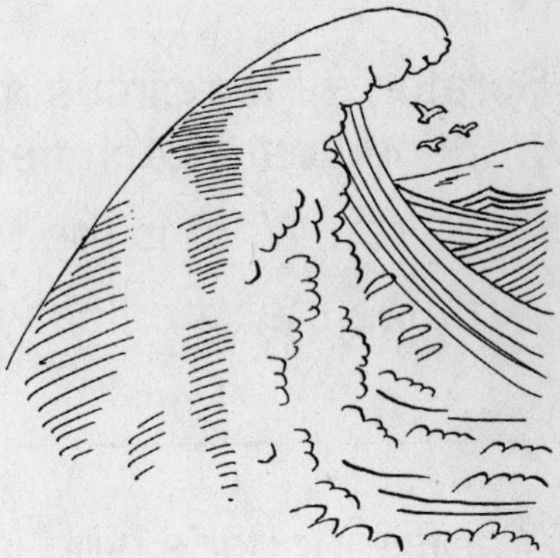

1. $0.08\overline{)1.12}$ T **2.** $5.5\overline{)38.5}$ I

3. $0.06\overline{)5.4}$ T **4.** $3.05\overline{)10.98}$ E

5. $\frac{5.6}{0.07}$ = ______ D **6.** $\frac{0.738}{0.82}$ = ______ S

7. 0.52 ÷ 13 = ______ I

8. 30.2 ÷ 6.04 = ______ B

9. 6.644 ÷ 3.02 = ______ I

10. 7.849 ÷ 0.5 = ______ P

Because ...

7 ______
14 ______

2.2 ______
0.9 ______

90 ______
0.04 ______
80 ______
3.6 ______

Use after pages 52–53.

NAME

Choose an Operation

SHARPEN YOUR SKILLS

For each problem below, tell whether you would use paper and pencil or a calculator. Then solve each problem and tell what operation you used.

1. Scratch's Flea circus has 30 working fleas. Each flea can jump $13\frac{1}{2}$ feet. What is the total distance that the fleas can jump?

2. An insect has six legs. A spider has eight. What is the total number of legs on one insect and one spider?

3. A grasshopper's hind leg is 3 times as long as its front leg. If its hind leg is 58.2 mm long, how long is its front leg?

4. A centipede has one pair of legs per body segment. If the centipede has 17 body segments, how many legs does it have?

5. A millipede has two pairs of legs per body segment. If the millipede has 18 body segments, how many legs does it have?

6. How many legs do one centipede and one millipede have together?

7. A tick has 8 legs. A flea has 6. What is the difference in the total number of legs of 6 ticks and 6 fleas?

8. A queen bee can lay 3,000 eggs per day. About how many eggs does she lay in 45 minutes?

9. About how many eggs would the queen bee lay in $16\frac{1}{4}$ hours?

10. What is the total number of legs among 8 ticks, 4 spiders, 3 fleas, and 4 grasshoppers?

NAME ________

SHARPEN YOUR SKILLS

Fractions and Decimals

Write each decimal as a fraction in lowest terms.

1. 0.7 = ______ **2.** 0.42 = ______ **3.** 0.035 = ______

4. 0.21 = ______ **5.** 0.54 = ______ **6.** 0.75 = ______

Write each fraction as a decimal.
Remember to put a bar over repeating decimals.

7. $\frac{11}{50}$ = ______ **8.** $\frac{3}{50}$ = ______ **9.** $\frac{33}{500}$ = ______

10. $\frac{9}{10}$ = ______ **11.** $\frac{12}{25}$ = ______ **12.** $\frac{9}{40}$ = ______

13. $\frac{29}{250}$ = ______ **14.** $\frac{4}{5}$ = ______ **15.** $\frac{1}{50}$ = ______

16. $\frac{7}{8}$ = ______ **17.** $\frac{2}{5}$ = ______ **18.** $\frac{3}{5}$ = ______

19. $\frac{7}{25}$ = ______ **20.** $\frac{11}{12}$ = ______ **21.** $\frac{1}{6}$ = ______

22. $\frac{3}{40}$ = ______ **23.** $\frac{9}{200}$ = ______ **24.** $\frac{8}{9}$ = ______

Solve the problem.

25. The diameter of a certain drill bit is 0.375 inch. What is the diameter of the drill bit if you write it as a fraction in lowest terms? ______

NAME

Fractions and Mixed Numbers

SHARPEN YOUR SKILLS

Write each mixed number as an improper fraction.

1. $7\frac{4}{5}$ = ________ 2. $3\frac{7}{9}$ = ________ 3. $6\frac{3}{8}$ = ________

4. $9\frac{7}{9}$ = ________ 5. $1\frac{4}{7}$ = ________ 6. $5\frac{1}{5}$ = ________

7. $5\frac{7}{8}$ = ________ 8. $4\frac{1}{3}$ = ________ 9. $8\frac{3}{5}$ = ________

Write each improper fraction as a whole number or a mixed number.

10. $\frac{17}{4}$ = ________ 11. $\frac{35}{8}$ = ________ 12. $\frac{96}{6}$ = ________

13. $\frac{43}{1}$ = ________ 14. $\frac{61}{12}$ = ________ 15. $\frac{240}{10}$ = ________

16. $\frac{19}{3}$ = ________ 17. $\frac{47}{7}$ = ________ 18. $\frac{71}{8}$ = ________

Compare these numbers. Use <, >, or =.

19. $8\frac{1}{2}$ ◯ $8\frac{5}{8}$ 20. $\frac{11}{12}$ ◯ $\frac{6}{7}$ 21. $1\frac{1}{3}$ ◯ $\frac{8}{9}$

22. $3\frac{7}{24}$ ◯ $2\frac{23}{24}$ 23. $2\frac{9}{13}$ ◯ $2\frac{18}{26}$ 24. $6\frac{5}{6}$ ◯ $6\frac{3}{4}$

List the numbers in order from least to greatest.

25. $3\frac{1}{2}$ $3\frac{9}{13}$ $3\frac{7}{26}$ ________________

26. $7\frac{5}{6}$ $7\frac{2}{3}$ $7\frac{11}{12}$ ________________

NAME

SHARPEN YOUR SKILLS

Estimating Sums and Differences of Fractions and Mixed Numbers

Round each number to the nearest half.

1. $\frac{1}{8}$ **2.** $3\frac{8}{9}$ **3.** $\frac{5}{6}$ **4.** $1\frac{3}{5}$ **5.** $\frac{3}{4}$ **6.** $\frac{3}{7}$

Estimate by comparing each fraction to the nearest half. Tell if the sum is greater than 1, less than 1, or greater than the larger fraction.

7. $\frac{5}{8} + \frac{1}{3}$ **8.** $\frac{1}{4} + \frac{1}{7}$ **9.** $\frac{5}{9} + \frac{3}{4}$ **10.** $\frac{9}{10} + \frac{7}{8}$ **11.** $\frac{1}{6} + \frac{3}{7}$

12. $\frac{3}{5} + \frac{6}{7}$ **13.** $\frac{3}{5} + \frac{1}{10}$ **14.** $\frac{7}{8} + \frac{2}{3}$ **15.** $\frac{1}{5} + \frac{7}{10}$ **16.** $\frac{1}{5} + \frac{1}{3}$

Find the range of each sum.

17. $2\frac{3}{8} + 5\frac{1}{6}$ **18.** $4\frac{4}{9} + 2$ **19.** $9\frac{1}{5} + 7$

Estimate by rounding to the nearest whole number.

20. $23\frac{5}{6} + 38\frac{2}{5}$ **21.** $90\frac{3}{8} - 12\frac{6}{7}$ **22.** $53\frac{1}{4} + 86\frac{3}{4}$

Estimate each sum or difference. Tell which method of estimation you used.

23. $42\frac{1}{3} + 10\frac{7}{9}$ **24.** $65 - 23\frac{1}{3}$

NAME

SHARPEN YOUR SKILLS

Adding and Subtracting Fractions and Mixed Numbers

Find the least common denominator.

1. $\frac{3}{7}, \frac{1}{3}$ ______ **2.** $\frac{2}{4}, \frac{1}{2}$ ______ **3.** $\frac{2}{6}, \frac{5}{8}$ ______ **4.** $\frac{2}{3}, \frac{3}{5}, \frac{2}{10}$ ______

Find the missing number.

5. $7 = \frac{\square}{2}$ **6.** $10\frac{1}{4} = \square\frac{5}{4}$ **7.** $4\frac{5}{8} = 3\frac{\square}{8}$

8. $5\frac{5}{8} = \frac{\square}{8}$ **9.** $12\frac{7}{8} = 11\frac{\square}{8}$ **10.** $1\frac{6}{7} = \square\frac{13}{7}$

Add or subtract. Write the answer in lowest terms.

11. $\frac{4}{9} - \frac{1}{3}$ ______ **12.** $\frac{13}{18} - \frac{1}{2}$ ______ **13.** $23\frac{3}{10} - 8\frac{1}{15}$ ______

14. $49\frac{11}{24} - 21\frac{1}{8}$ ______ **15.** $6\frac{7}{12} - \frac{1}{3}$ ______ **16.** $5\frac{1}{4} - 3\frac{1}{5}$ ______

17. $28\frac{3}{10} - 26\frac{1}{3}$ ______ **18.** $7\frac{5}{16} - 3\frac{3}{4}$ ______ **19.** $20\frac{1}{4} - 17$ ______

20. $3\frac{1}{3} + 6\frac{1}{9}$ ______ **21.** $\frac{1}{5} + \frac{1}{2} + \frac{1}{10}$ ______ **22.** $9\frac{4}{5} + 3\frac{1}{3} + 6\frac{1}{6}$ ______

Mental Math Use mental math to find each missing number.

23. $\frac{5}{8} + \frac{\square}{8} = 1$ **24.** $1\frac{3}{4} - \frac{\square}{\square} = 1\frac{5}{12}$ **25.** $7\frac{2}{5} + \frac{\square}{\square} = 8$

Use after pages 66–69.

NAME

SHARPEN YOUR SKILLS

Multiplying and Dividing Fractions and Mixed Numbers

Multiply or divide. **Remember** to multiply by the reciprocal in division.

1. $\frac{2}{3} \times \frac{3}{2} \times \frac{1}{5}$

2. $\frac{15}{16} \times \frac{4}{5} \times \frac{1}{3}$

3. $\frac{7}{16} \times \frac{4}{7} \times \frac{2}{3}$

4. $\frac{1}{2} \times \frac{2}{3} \times \frac{3}{4}$

5. $4\frac{2}{3} \times \frac{1}{14}$

6. $9 \div 1\frac{1}{2}$

7. $\frac{5}{16} \div 1\frac{5}{8}$

8. $2\frac{3}{4} \times 2\frac{3}{4}$

9. $1\frac{9}{12} \div 1\frac{4}{5}$

10. $12 \div 5\frac{1}{3}$

11. $(5\frac{2}{3})(2\frac{1}{10})$

12. $\frac{7}{8} \div \frac{3}{16}$

13. $(4\frac{2}{3})(\frac{1}{14})(\frac{1}{2})$

14. $\frac{2}{3} \div 2\frac{2}{5}$

15. $10\frac{1}{2} \times 1\frac{5}{7}$

16. $\frac{3}{8} \div \frac{3}{16}$

17. $1\frac{5}{6} \times 12\frac{3}{4}$

18. $6 \div 1\frac{3}{16}$

Mixed Practice Compute each answer.

19. $4\frac{3}{8} \times 7\frac{5}{7}$

20. $\frac{7}{8} - \frac{3}{7}$

21. $\frac{7}{10} + 21\frac{1}{4}$

NAME

SHARPEN YOUR SKILLS

Too Much or Too Little Information

The New York City Transit Authority operates the world's largest subway system. The Transit Authority maintains 370 km of track that carries approximately one-half million passengers per day. The cost to construct the subway, which opened in 1897, was about $1.6 million per kilometer.

Solve each problem. If there is not enough information to solve, write *too little information.*

1. How many miles are in the Montreal subway system?

____

2. About how many trains run each day in the New York subway system?

____

3. What was the approximate total cost of the New York City subway system?

____

4. To the nearest tenth of a mile, what is the average depth of the subway?

____

5. For how many years has the New York City subway system been in operation through 1990?

____

6. What is the annual cost of operating the New York City subway?

____

NAME

SHARPEN YOUR SKILLS

Meaning of Integers

Answer each question.

1. If 37 represents an increase of 37 degrees, what does −37 represent?

2. If −16 represents a loss of 16 pounds, what does 7 represent?

3. If −15 represents a withdrawal of $15, what does 42 represent?

4. If 72 represents miles north, what does −38 represent?

Write an integer for each exercise. **Remember** to write a negative sign for negative integers.

5. A loss of 10 pounds ______
6. 4 inches taller ______
7. 24 degrees below zero ______
8. A loss of 9 yards ______
9. A profit of $32 ______
10. A gain of 6 pounds ______
11. $|57|$ ______
12. $|-16|$ ______
13. 5 strokes over par ______
14. 7 inches shorter ______
15. The opposite of −25 ______
16. The opposite of 12 ______
17. $|-(26)|$ ______
18. $-(-91)$ ______
19. An altitude of 7,000 feet ______
20. 20,000 leagues below sea level ______
21. 22 units to the right of zero on the number line ______
22. 14 units to the left of zero on the number line ______

Use after pages 84–85.

NAME ____________

Adding and Subtracting Integers

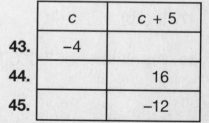

SHARPEN YOUR SKILLS

Add or subtract.

1. $-4 - (4)$ ____
2. $-7 + 9$ ____
3. $-9 - (-9)$ ____
4. $-25 - (-5)$ ____
5. $0 + (-8)$ ____
6. $-8 - (-12)$ ____
7. $-9 + 22$ ____
8. $-17 - 20$ ____
9. $15 - 42$ ____
10. $-12 + (-2)$ ____
11. $67 - (-66)$ ____
12. $13 + (-7)$ ____
13. $6 - 26$ ____
14. $-22 - 15$ ____
15. $-32 - (-36)$ ____
16. $14 + (-20)$ ____
17. $8 - (-7)$ ____
18. $8 + (-3)$ ____
19. $-9 + 9 =$ ____
20. $37 - 22$ ____
21. $-15 + 8$ ____
22. $17 + (-7)$ ____
23. $-12 + 8$ ____
24. $-36 - (-9)$ ____
25. $9 - (-4)$ ____
26. $-9 + (-9)$ ____
27. $16 + (-2)$ ____
28. $24 - (-10)$ ____
29. $-32 + 27$ ____
30. $16 + (-32)$ ____
31. $-10 + 28 + (-7)$ ____
32. $-19 + 21 + 15 + (-5)$ ____
33. $32 - 54 - (-2)$ ____
34. $61 - (-50) + 22$ ____
35. $-4 - 8 - (-12)$ ____
36. $-38 - 21 - (-51)$ ____

Complete the tables.

	a	$9 + a$
37.	2	
38.	−2	
39.	−3	

	b	$12 - b$
40.		7
41.	0	
42.		−4

	c	$c + 5$
43.	−4	
44.		16
45.		−12

NAME

SHARPEN YOUR SKILLS

Multiplying and Dividing Integers

Multiply and divide.

1. 54 ÷ 6 ______
2. 4(2)(3)(– 3) ______
3. $(-3)^3$ ______
4. (– 56) ÷ 7 ______
5. 35 ÷ (– 7) ______
6. (– 30) ÷ (– 6) ______
7. 45 ÷ (– 9) ______
8. (– 48) ÷ (– 12) ______
9. (– 6)(– 3)(4)(– 7) ______
10. 6(4)(– 8)(– 3)(4) ______
11. (–40) ÷ (–5) ______
12. 0 ÷ 15 ______
13. (–48) ÷ (–16) ______
14. (–50) ÷ (–5) ______
15. (–35) ÷ 7 ______
16. (– 5)(18) ______
17. $(-6)^2$ ______
18. (–765) ÷ 85 ______
19. (–1,026) ÷ (–171) ______
20. (400)(–12)(3) ______

Solve each problem.

21. A club wants to collect $1,500 in ticket sales for a film festival. They expect to sell 375 tickets. How much should they charge for each ticket?

______

22. The club charges $3 for tickets sold in advance. They sold 165 tickets in advance. How much did the club collect in advance sales?

______

NAME

SHARPEN YOUR SKILLS

Use Data from a Table

Number of wrong answers \ Number of right answers	0	1	2	3	4	5	6	7	8
0	0	15	30	45	60	75	90	105	120
1	−5	10	25	40	55	70	85	100	
2	−10	5	20	35	50	65	80		
3	−15	0	15	30	45	60			
4	−20	−5	10	25	40				
5	−25	−10	5	20					
6	−30	−15	0						
7	−35	−20							
8	−40								

This table shows the scores that are possible for an 8-item test. 15 points are given for each right answer and 5 points are subtracted for each wrong answer.

Use the table to solve each problem.

1. David's score was 105. How many test items did he get right?

____

2. Karina answered 6 questions. What are the highest and lowest scores she can earn?

____

3. Can someone score 80 points if he or she gets 4 items wrong?

____

4. Jeanette's score was 100. How many wrong answers did she have?

____

5. Darrin answered 3 questions incorrectly. How many would he have to get right to score more than 45 points?

____

6. A passing score is 50. If someone had 4 right answers, what is the greatest number of wrong answers he or she can have and still pass?

____

NAME

SHARPEN YOUR SKILLS

Meaning of Rational Numbers

Write each rational number as the quotient of two integers.

1. -12 ______________________ **2.** 7.3 ______________________

3. $-2\frac{2}{7}$ ______________________ **4.** $5\frac{1}{3}$ ______________________

List the numbers in order from least to greatest.

5. $\frac{3}{-5}$ $\frac{-1}{4}$ $\frac{-1}{8}$

____

6. $\frac{1}{-8}$ $\frac{-1}{7}$ $\frac{-1}{9}$

____

7. $\frac{-6}{-2}$ -6 $\frac{-3}{2}$

____

8. $\frac{-2}{-5}$ 3 $\frac{-2}{-10}$

____

From START to END, shade a path that always leads to a greater number.

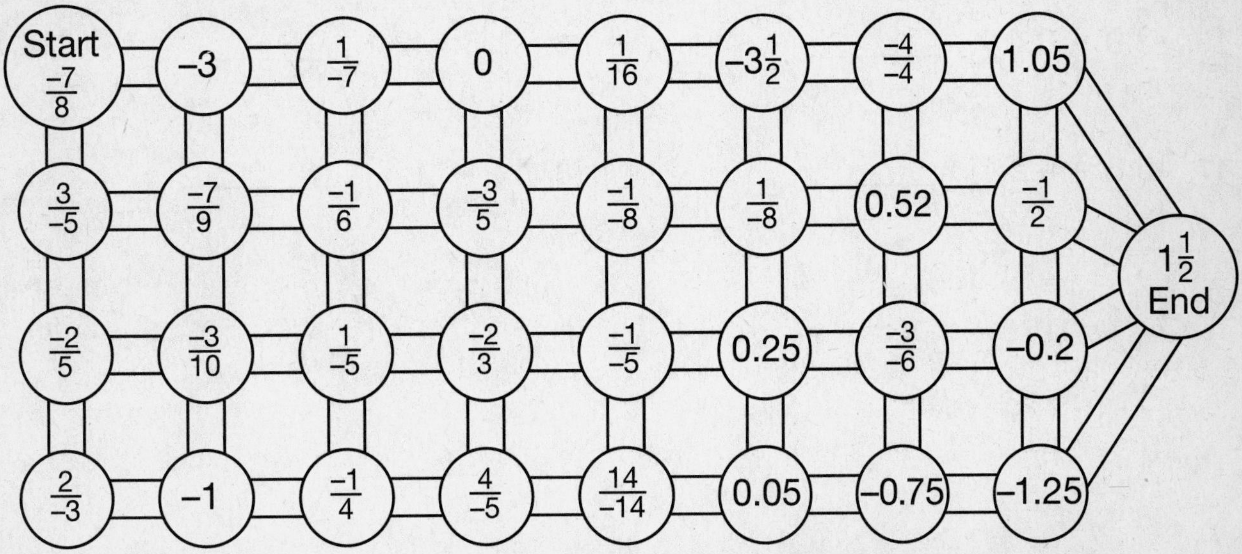

NAME ______

SHARPEN YOUR SKILLS

Adding and Subtracting Rational Numbers

Add or subtract. **Remember** to add the opposite when you need to subtract.

1. $-\frac{5}{6} + (-\frac{1}{3})$ ______

2. $-\frac{5}{8} + \frac{2}{3}$ ______

3. $-\frac{2}{7} + (-\frac{1}{3})$ ______

4. $-\frac{7}{8} - (-\frac{1}{3})$ ______

5. $\frac{3}{5} - \frac{1}{8}$ ______

6. $2\frac{1}{2} - (-\frac{5}{14})$ ______

7. $-5 + (-\frac{4}{7})$ ______

8. $4 - (-\frac{2}{3})$ ______

9. $0 - \frac{4}{5}$ ______

10. $-6 - (-\frac{3}{4})$ ______

11. $-\frac{1}{2} + 3$ ______

12. $5 + (-\frac{9}{11})$ ______

13. $-6.3 - (-1.8)$ ______

14. $0.6 - 0.91$ ______

15. $-2.9 - 0.4$ ______

16. $-1.3 + 2.1$ ______

17. $-5.6 - (-2.1)$ ______

18. $1.2 - 1.4$ ______

NAME

SHARPEN YOUR SKILLS

Multiplying and Dividing Rationals

What is a wet mutt?

To find out, work each exercise. Find each answer below and cross out the letter with it. Write the remaining letters on the blanks at the bottom.

Multiply or divide.

1. $-\frac{3}{7}(\frac{7}{9})$ = ______
2. $\frac{6}{7} \div (-\frac{3}{21})$ = ______
3. $\frac{5}{6} \div (-\frac{5}{6})$ = ______
4. $-9(-\frac{4}{18})$ = ______
5. $1 \div (-\frac{1}{4})$ = ______
6. $(-\frac{2}{9})(-\frac{2}{3})$ = ______
7. $-\frac{4}{5}(\frac{3}{8})$ = ______
8. $-\frac{5}{12} \div \frac{8}{9}$ = ______
9. $-\frac{2}{5} \div (-\frac{7}{10})$ = ______
10. $-5(0.4)$ = ______
11. $-1.3(-2.1)$ = ______
12. $4.4(-3.5)$ = ______
13. $-10 \div 2.5$ = ______
14. $8 \div 0.5$ = ______
15. $-4.5 \div 0.9$ = ______

-4	13	-1	$-\frac{1}{3}$	$-\frac{3}{10}$	16	-2	$-\frac{2}{5}$	-15.4
M	I	T	C	G	Y	P	T	T
-13	$\frac{4}{27}$	$\frac{5}{28}$	$-\frac{15}{32}$	2	9	$-\frac{4}{27}$	1	-4
S	R	A	D	S	S	O	G	I
-5	$\frac{1}{10}$	2.73	-7	-6	$\frac{2.4}{2.5}$	$\frac{4}{7}$	$\frac{3}{5}$	10
T	G	G	Y	I	D	W	O	G

___ ___'___ ___ ___ ___ ___ ___ ___ ___ ___ ___!

NAME

SHARPEN YOUR SKILLS

Use a Formula

Tell which formula you would use to find the corresponding temperature on the other scale. Then find and label your answer in the appropriate scale.

$F = \frac{9}{5}C + 32$ $C = \frac{5}{9}(F - 32)$

1. 23° F

2. 20° C

3. 194° F

4. 77° C

5. 60° C

6. 14° F

7. 50° F

8. –20° C

9. –100° C

10. 113° F

11. –45° C

12. 104° F

13. 1,000° C

14. –4° F

15. –200° C

Use after pages 100–101.

NAME

SHARPEN YOUR SKILLS

Order of Operations

Compute. Use mental math or paper and pencil.

1. $4 + 3 \times 6$ ______

2. $8^2 \times 3 - 5$ ______

3. $17 - 4 \times 3 + 18$ ______

4. $9^2 + 4^2 - (8 \times 2)$ ______

5. $(13 - 8) - 2^2$ ______

6. $\frac{(12^2 - 44) \times 3}{5^2 \times 2} + 134$ ______

7. $\frac{(4^3 \div 8) \times 6}{(3^2 \div 3)} - 4$ ______

8. $\frac{(54 \div 3^2) \times 4}{6 \times 2} \div 2$ ______

9. $\frac{46 - 6 \times 7}{2^2} + 25$ ______

10. $8 \times 3 \div 6 + 6^2 + 90 + 5$ ______

Insert parentheses in each of the following so that the given equations are true.

11. $\frac{14^2 - 80 \times 2}{3 \times 2} = 6$

12. $9 \div 3 + 6 \times 2 = 2$

13. $6^2 + 6^2 \div 4 - 30 = 15$

14. $44 \div 11 + 15^2 \div 5 - 7^2 = 0$

15. $\frac{9 \times 8 - 1^2 + 1^2}{2 \times 2 + 1} = 14$

16. $\frac{96 \div 2 \div 9 + 3}{5} \times 10 = 8$

17. $\frac{6^2 - 2 \div 20 - 3}{2^2} = 0.5$

18. $\frac{9 \times 3 + 5 - 2 \times 3}{9 \times 4 + 1 - 27} = 2$

Solve each problem.

19. When the basketball team went out to eat, the coach paid for 12 hamburgers at $1.69 each and 13 cups of milk at 69¢ each. Which expression shows how much he paid?

______

a. (12 × $.69) + (13 × $1.69)
b. (12 × $1.69) + (13 × $.69)
c. (12 + 13) × ($.69 + $1.69)

20. Fourteen children, 6 adults, and 5 senior citizens are riding the train through the park. An adult ticket costs $1.50. Children and senior citizens can ride for $1.25. Write an expression which shows the total in ticket fares.

______

______

NAME

SHARPEN YOUR SKILLS

Evaluating Expressions

Evaluate each expression when $x = 6$, $y = \frac{1}{3}$, and $z = -2$. **Remember** to do the operations within the parentheses first.

1. $3x$ ______

2. $5x$ ______

3. $6y$ ______

4. $x + z$ ______

5. $5x + 3y$ ______

6. $3(x + z)$ ______

7. $\frac{2x}{z}$ ______

8. $z(x + y)$ ______

9. $x(x + 2y)$ ______

10. $5x - z$ ______

11. $z(2x + y)$ ______

12. $x^2 + xy$ ______

Evaluate $2a + 5c$ when

13. $a = \frac{1}{2}$ and $c = \frac{1}{4}$. ______

14. $a = 2\frac{1}{4}$ and $c = \frac{5}{8}$. ______

15. $a = 1.6$ and $c = 3.7$. ______

16. $a = 2.1$ and $c = 3.2$. ______

Tell whether the sentence is true for $f = 2$ and for $f = 10$.

17. $2f + 1 + 2f = 5f$ ______

18. $3f + 5 = 5f + 1$ ______

19. $f + 2f = 3f$ ______

20. $2f^2 = 20f + 160$ ______

NAME

SHARPEN YOUR SKILLS

Writing Expressions and Equations

Write a mathematical expression for each exercise.

1. k added to 8 ________

2. t decreased by 50 ________

3. 60 less than xy ________

4. y^3 increased by 7 ________

5. 68 divided by z ________

6. w divided by 6 ________

7. The product of d^2 and 15 ________

8. b multiplied by 142 ________

For each table, choose the correct equation.

9.

x	0	1	2	3	4
y	5	8	11	14	17

a. $y = 2x + 1$ **b.** $y = x + 5$ **c.** $y = 3x + 5$

10.

x	0	10	20	30
y	3	23	43	63

a. $y = 2x + 3$ **b.** $y = 2x - 3$ **c.** $y = 3x - 7$

Tell whether the sentence is true, false, or open.

11. $-3 < -4$ ________

12. $9 = 32 + x$ ________

13. $7 + 1 < 9$ ________

14. $9 = x + 5$ ________

Write a mathematical expression for each problem.

15. Sixty students from Polk Junior High School spent a weekend at a computer camp. They traveled to the camp in c buses. How many students rode in each bus?

____

16. At the camp, 4 students shared 1 computer. Each student used the computer n hours over the weekend. How many total hours was the computer used?

____

Use after pages 120–121.

NAME

SHARPEN YOUR SKILLS

Writing and Solving Addition/Subtraction One-Step Equations

Solve each equation. **Remember** to check your solution.

1. $s + 8 = 5$ __________

2. $-6 + x = -13$ __________

3. $3 = t - 5$ __________

4. $b - 8 = -5$ __________

5. $r + 3.2 = -6$ __________

6. $13 + w = -155$ __________

7. $-6 + x = 3.4$ __________

8. $3.2 = 6.7 + k$ __________

9. $t - (-7) = 5$ __________

10. $w + \frac{3}{4} = 2\frac{1}{2}$ __________

11. $s - \frac{4}{7} = -\frac{2}{3}$ __________

12. $-\frac{7}{8} + m = -\frac{2}{5}$ __________

13. $\frac{3}{8} + w = \frac{3}{4}$ __________

14. $t - (-0.3) = -0.6$ __________

15. $\frac{5}{12} + f = -2$ __________

Write and solve an equation for each problem.

16. 19 blue marbles are added to a jar of mixed marbles making a total of 57 marbles. How many mixed marbles were in the jar?

____

____

17. If 321.6 is subtracted from a number, the result is 15.8. What is the number?

____

____

NAME

SHARPEN YOUR SKILLS

Solving One-Step Multiplication/ Division Equations

Solve each equation.

1. $45 = \frac{n}{5}$

2. $2.4x = 1.8$

3. $\frac{1}{3}y = 14$

4. $\frac{18}{5} = \frac{4m}{3}$

5. $\frac{2}{3}n = -18$

6. $40p = 1{,}520$

7. $5q = -4\frac{2}{3}$

8. $7r = -\frac{7}{8}$

9. $2\frac{5}{7}t = 10$

10. $10x = 24$

11. $1\frac{1}{3}p = 18$

12. $63q = 1{,}071$

Mixed Practice Solve each equation.

13. $k + 7 = 34$

14. $\frac{1}{4} + g = \frac{5}{8}$

15. $x - 81 = 53$

16. $1\frac{1}{2} + t = 4$

17. $3\frac{1}{4}y = 2\frac{1}{2}$

18. $6 = 3\frac{1}{2} + b$

NAME

SHARPEN YOUR SKILLS

Write an Equation

Write and solve an equation for each problem. **Remember** to do the same thing to both sides of the equation.

1. Stacy spent $\frac{3}{4}$ of her money at the fair. She spent \$9. How much money did she have?

2. Will worked from 10 A.M. to 6 P.M. and earned \$30. How much did he earn per hour?

3. A new baseball glove costs \$30. How many weeks must Ryan work to save enough money to buy the glove, if he earns \$7.50 per week?

4. Marie has \$4.75 to spend at the movies. Her ticket costs \$3. How much money will she have to spend on snacks?

5. One fourth of the students are members of the Pep Club. If there are 193 members, how many students are in the school?

6. A crowd of 528 students attended the basketball game. This is $\frac{4}{5}$ of the students. What is the total number of students in school?

7. Ruth earns \$48 a day at a rate of \$6 per hour. How many hours does she work each day?

8. Laura works for 14 hours and earns \$105. How much does she earn per hour?

NAME

Writing and Solving Two-Step Equations

SHARPEN YOUR SKILLS

Ez Word Riddles—two letters solve each riddle.

First riddle:
A baseball player who struck out is ____ ____

Second riddle:
Something cold and slippery is: ____ ____

To solve the riddles, solve each equation. In the chart below, cross out each box containing a solution. The remaining letters solve the riddles.

1. $\frac{e}{3} + 97 = 100$ ________

2. $8e + 43 = 91$ ________

3. $43 + 10e = 73$ ________

4. $36 + \frac{e}{2} = 40$ ________

5. $200 = 56 + 12e$ ________

6. $\frac{e}{13} + 141 = 144$ ________

7. $950 + \frac{z}{2} = 987$ ________

8. $100 = 9e + 37$ ________

9. $600 = 416 + 46e$ ________

10. $\frac{z}{2} + 432 = 543$ ________

11. $237 = 61 + 16z$ ________

12. $11z - 45 = 65$ ________

13. $120 = 4z + 56$ ________

14. $24z - 88 = 32$ ________

15. $4z - 24 = 28$ ________

16. $200 = 4z + 68$ ________

First Riddle	4 T	9 D	74 A	15 K	13 L	222 K	8 R	66 C	39 M	16 B
Second Riddle	10 S	3 H	7 J	5 R	6 N	17 I	11 M	12 Y	33 E	999 C

Use after pages 130–131.

NAME

SHARPEN YOUR SKILLS

Write an Equation

Write an equation and solve each problem.

1. Steven must save $240 to attend summer camp next year. He has already saved $30. If he earns $14 per week, how many weeks must he save in order to have the money he needs for summer camp?

2. Kelly purchased two tapes at the music store in the mall. She gave the clerk a $20 bill and received $1.60 in change. If the tapes were priced the same, how much did the store charge for each?

3. In another store at the mall, Kelly bought a sweater. She also bought three pairs of pants that cost $24 each. The total cost of these purchases was $100. How much was the sweater?

4. At the snack bar, two hamburgers and two orders of fries cost $5.20. If an order of fries costs $.60, what is the cost of a hamburger?

5. Mrs. Rivera purchased a gold chain and three pairs of earrings at the jewelry store. The total cost of her purchase was $220. If the gold chain cost $70 and each pair of earrings was priced the same, what was the cost of each pair?

6. Paul bought 2 shirts, each at the same price. He also bought a tie for $12. If he paid a total of $57, what was the price of each shirt?

NAME

SHARPEN YOUR SKILLS

Graphing Equations and Inequalities

Graph each equation or inequality on the number line provided.

1. $a < 4$

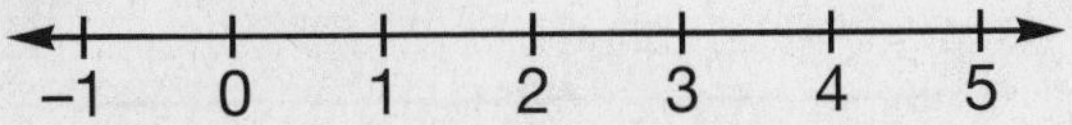

2. $b \geq -1$

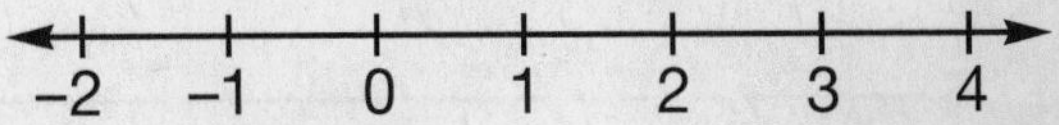

3. $c \leq 1$ and $c > -3$

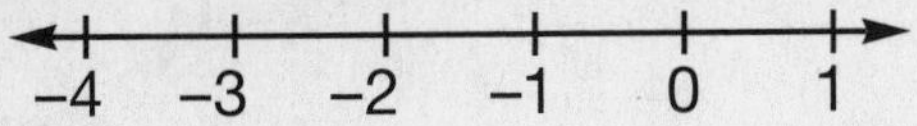

4. $d < -0.5$

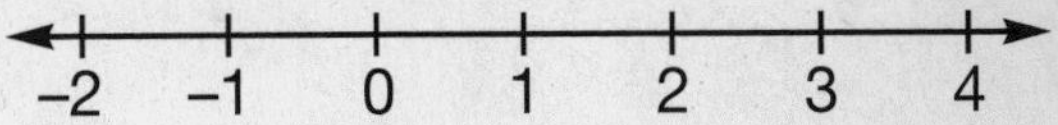

5. $f > \frac{1}{2}$ or $f < 4$

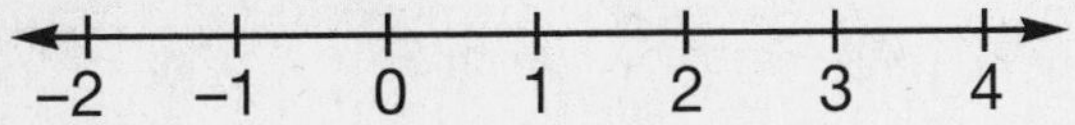

6. $g = -6$

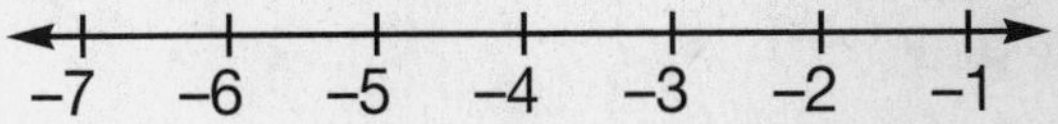

Write an inequality for each graph.

7.

____

8.
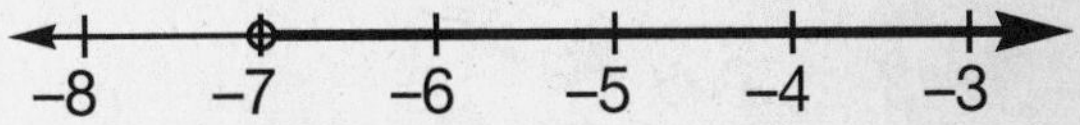

____

9.
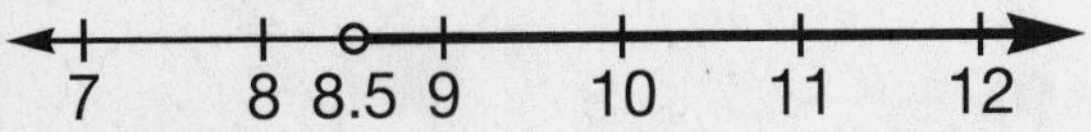

____

10.
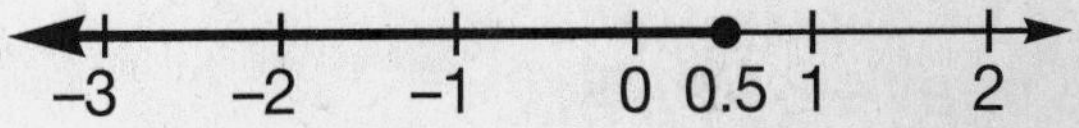

____

Solve the problem.

11. The altitude of Mt. Everest is 5.5 miles. Write an inequality to express the heights of all altitudes higher than Mt. Everest.

____

12. The depth of the Mariana Trench is –6.9 miles, and the depth of the Brazil Basin is –3.8 miles. Write an inequality to express all depths between the two.

____

NAME

Solving Inequalities by Graphing

SHARPEN YOUR SKILLS

Write each solution as an inequality.

1. $x + 3 > 4$

2. $\frac{1}{2}t \geq -1$

3. $-m + 5 > -3$

4. $-2x < -4$

5. $y + 7 > 2$

6. $-5y > -35$

7. $-x + 5 < -2$

8. $c - 12 > 20$

9. $a - 6 < -4$

10. $-y - 5 \leq 9$

11. $m + 6 \geq -8$

12. $9 \leq -7 + g$

13. $-7 + \ -f < -5.5$

14. $0 \leq -a - 6.7$

Use after pages 148–149.

NAME

SHARPEN YOUR SKILLS

Use a Diagram

In Burgerton, locations are given as east or west of Chili Ave., and north or south of Mustard Street. The distance between each group of 600 street numbers is 1 mile.

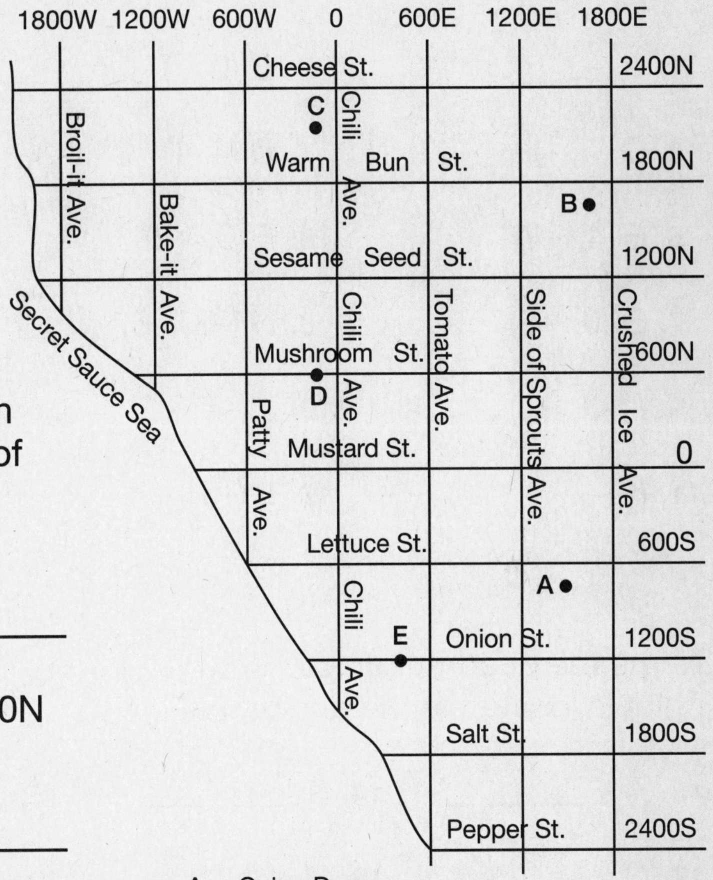

A. Onion Dome
B. Lemonade's Last Stand
C. Styrofoam Factory
D. Vinegar Distillery
E. Cholesterol Screening Clinic

1. Give the location of the Onion Dome Stadium east or west of Chili, and north or south of Mustard.

____

2. What streets intersect at 1800N and 1200W?

____

Estimation For each location, give the street number east or west of Chili, and north or south of Mustard.

3. Intersection of Mushroom and Patty

____

4. Intersection of Lettuce and Tomato

____

Tell what is on the map at the given distances from Mustard and Chili.

5. $\frac{1}{4}$ mi west and 1 mi north

____

6. $\frac{1}{2}$ mi east and 2 mi south

____

____

NAME

SHARPEN YOUR SKILLS

Graphing in the Coordinate Plane

Plot the points on the coordinate grid and connect them in order *A-L* and then *L* to *A*.

1. *A* (–3, 5) **2.** *B* (0, 5)

3. *C* (0, 1) **4.** *D* (4, 1)

5. *E* (4, –2) **6.** *F* (0, –2)

7. *G* (0, –6) **8.** *H* (–3, –6)

9. *I* (–3, –2) **10.** *J* (–7, –2)

11. *K* (–7, 1) **12.** *L* (–3, 1)

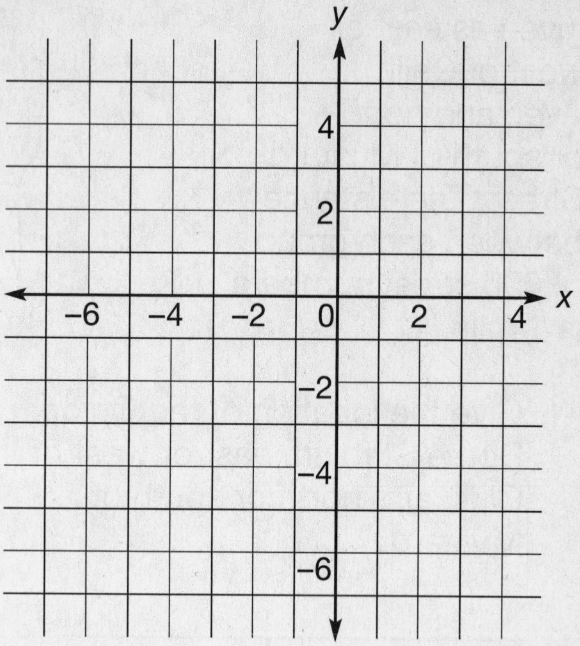

Name the quadrant or axis in which each point is located in the diagram above.

13. *A* ________ **14.** *B* ________ **15.** *D* ________ **16.** *E* ________

17. *G* ________ **18.** *H* ________ **19.** *J* ________ **20.** *K* ________

Graph the three lines on the same coordinate grid.

21. $y = x + 1$; $y = -x + 4$; $y = x + 3$

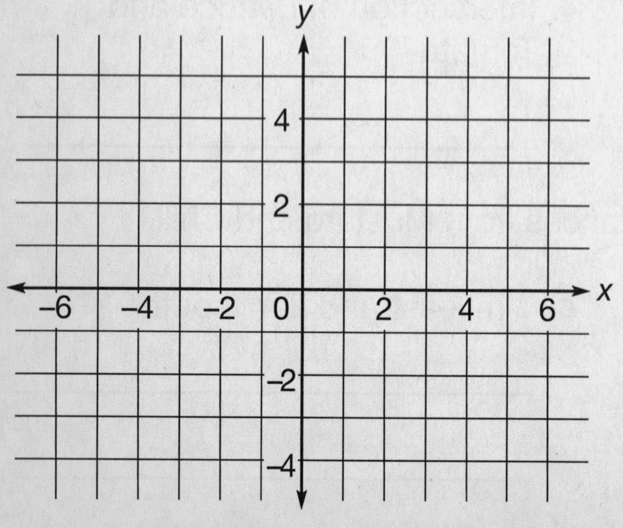

22. $y = 2x + 2$; $y = -x$; $y = -\frac{1}{3}x - 3$

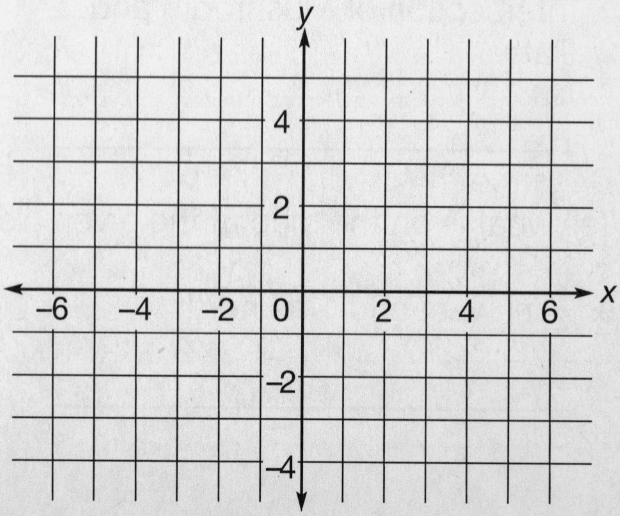

NAME

SHARPEN YOUR SKILLS

Graphing Pairs of Linear Equations

Graph each pair of equations on the same grid.

1. $y = \frac{1}{2}x + 3$
$y = \frac{1}{2}x - 1$

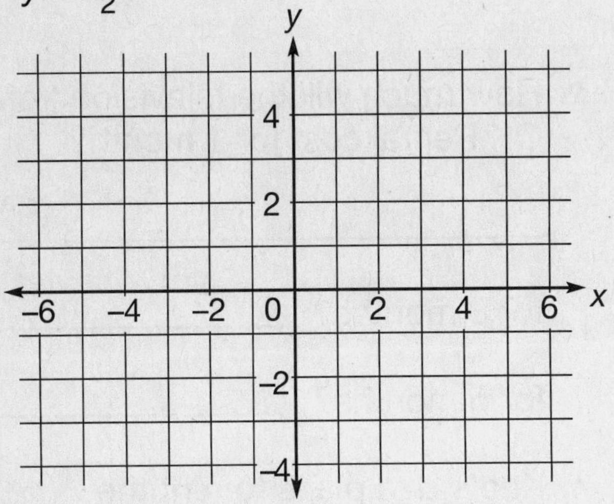

2. $y = -2x + 1$
$y = 2x + 1$

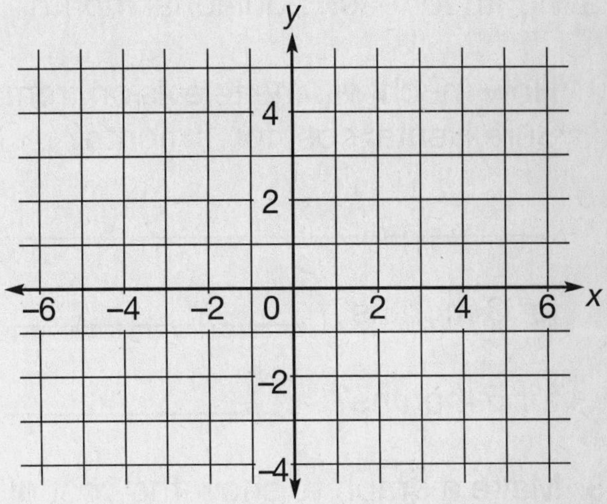

3. $y = 3x + 2$
$y = -x - 3$

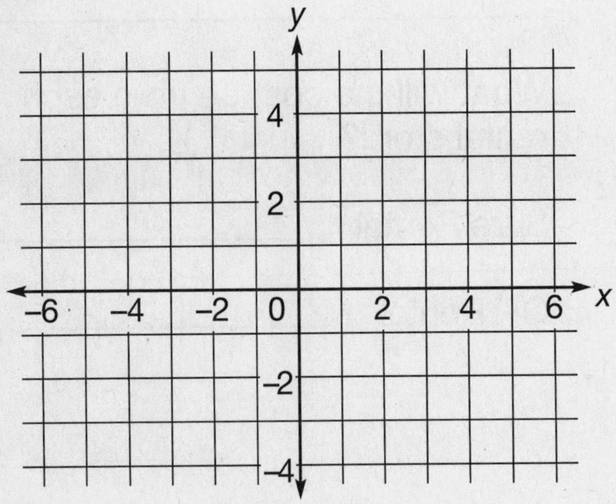

4. $y = 3x + 1$
$y = -2x + 4$

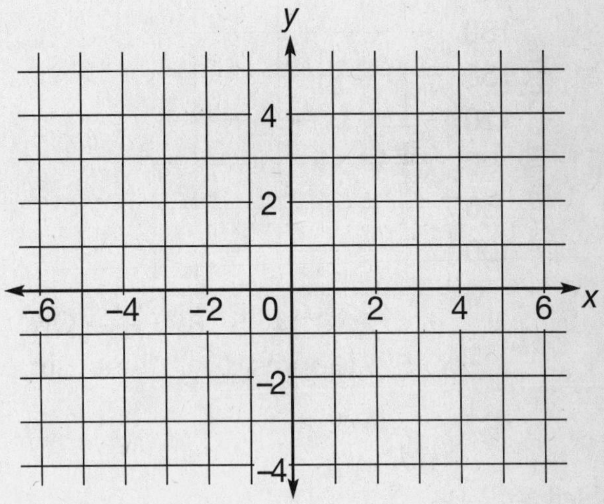

Describe the graphs in

5. Exercise 1.

____

____

6. Exercise 2.

____

____

NAME

Make a Graph

SHARPEN YOUR SKILLS

Kao's dad can rent a television from Sure Rental for $30 a month. He can rent a television from OK Rental for $100 for a minimum of 3 months rental, and then $25 a month for each additional month.

1. How much will the television from Sure Rental cost for 1 month? ____________

   for 3 months? ____________

   for 5 months? ____________

2. How much will the television from OK Rental cost for 1 month? ____________

   for 3 months? ____________

   for 5 mo...

3. Mak...

   th...

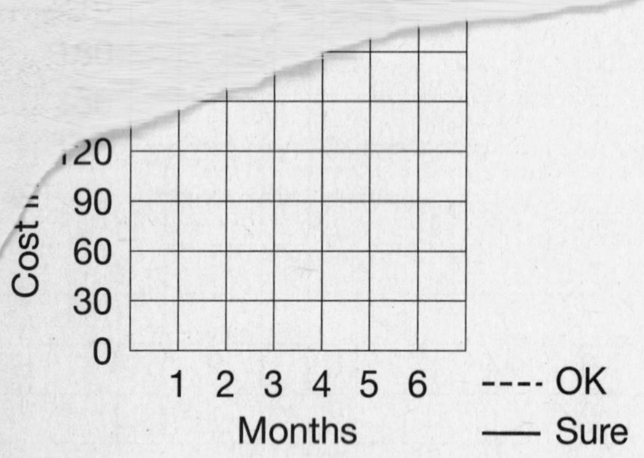

____

What will the cost be from each rental store?

Sure Rental ____________

OK Rental ____________

Solve.

5. Kelly had $25 and started saving $5 per week. Kristen had $20 and started saving $7.50 per week. When did Kelly have more money saved than Kristen?

   ____

6. When did Kristen have more money saved than Kelly?

   ____

NAME

SHARPEN YOUR SKILLS

Writing Equations from Graphs

For each exercise, write an equation that fits the data.

1.

x	y
11	16
10	15
0	5
–1	4

2.

x	y
27	9
18	6
15	5
3	1

3.

x	y
21	3
14	2
7	1
0	0
–28	–4

4.

x	y
10	9
8	7
5	4
2	1
1	0

5.

x	y
5	8
3	6
1	4
–1	2
–3	0

6.

x	y
4	0
2	–2
0	–4
–2	–6
–3	–7

7.

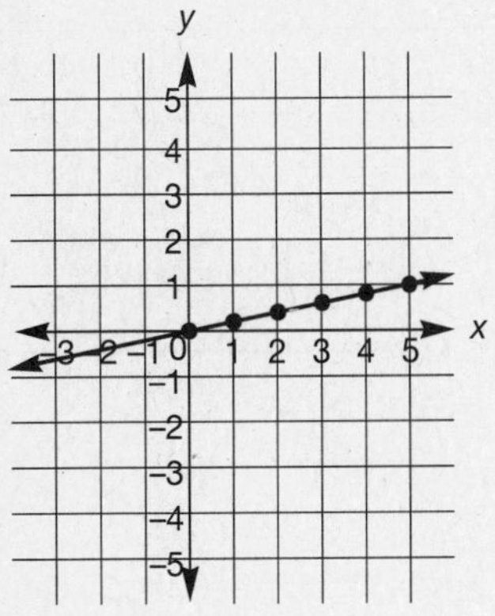

8.

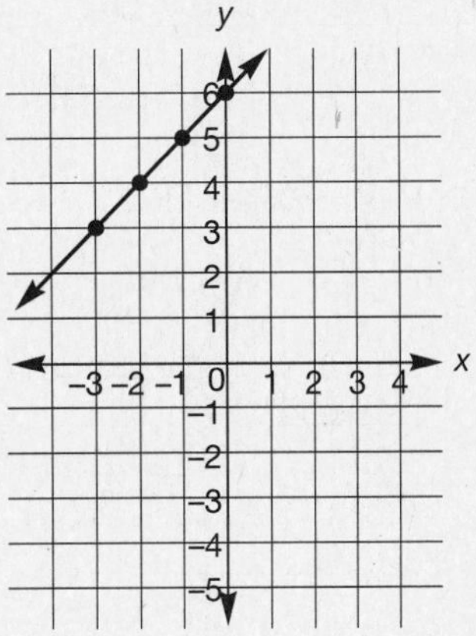

9.

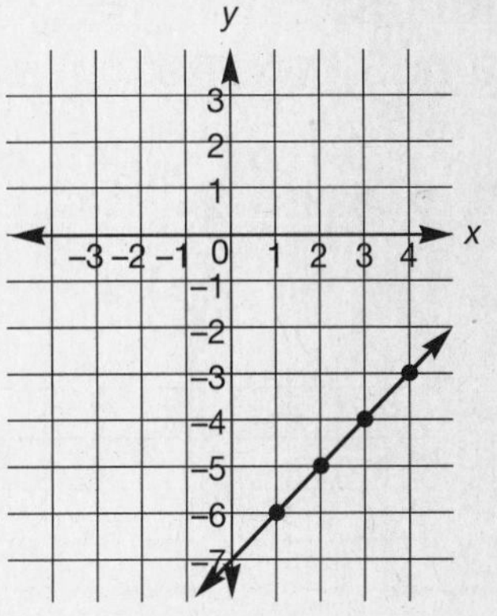

NAME

SHARPEN YOUR SKILLS

Graphing Inequalities in Four Quadrants

Graph each inequality on a coordinate grid.

1. $y > -3x$

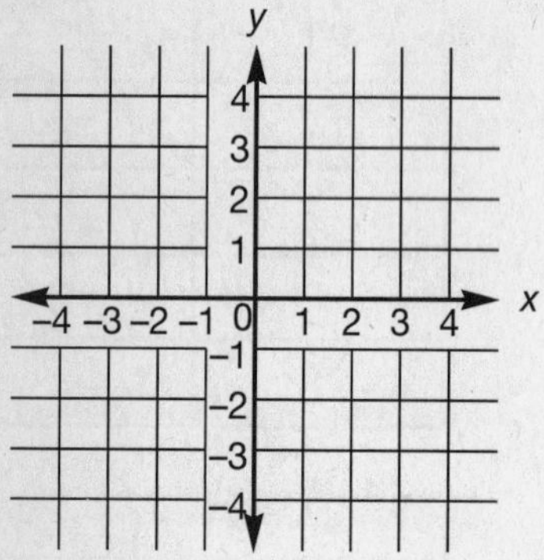

2. $y \leq x + 2$

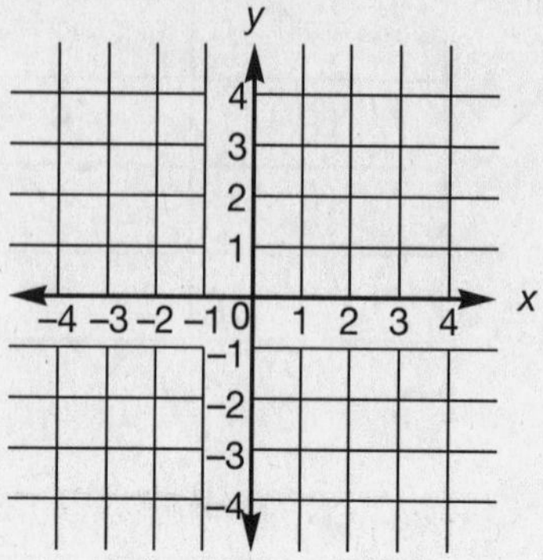

3. $y < x + 3$

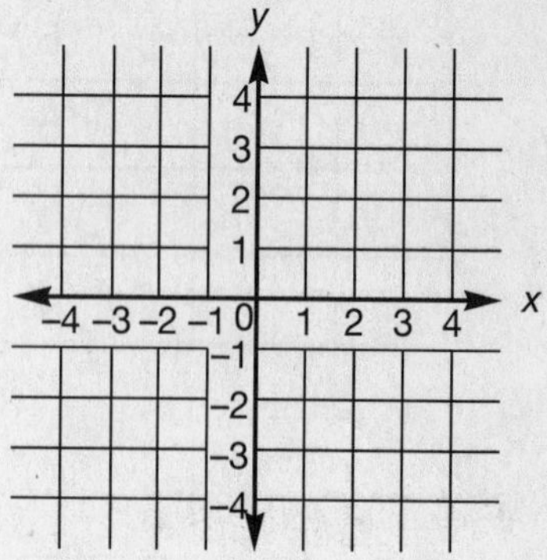

4. $y > -x$

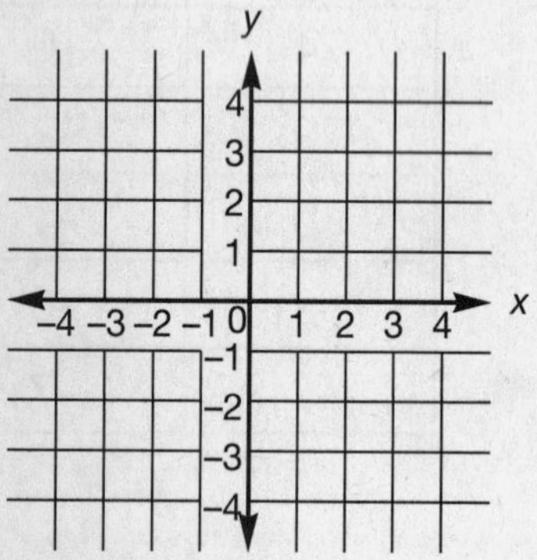

5. $y < x - 1$

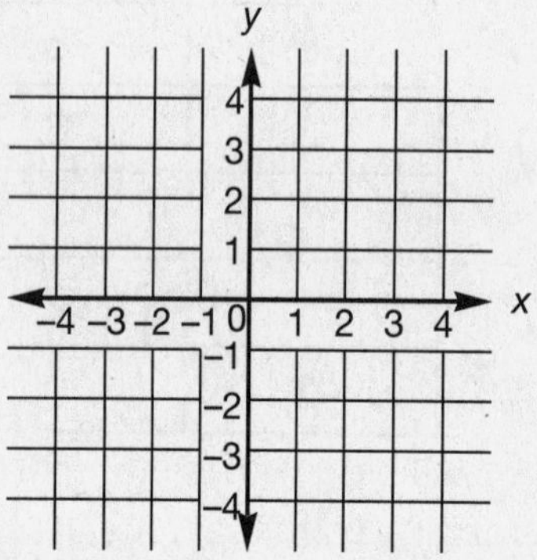

6. $y \leq 3x$

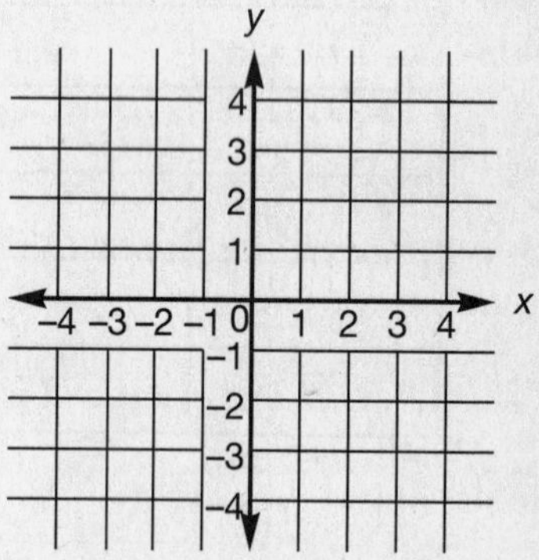

Mixed Practice Graph each inequality on a coordinate grid or a number line.

7. $y \geq x - 2$

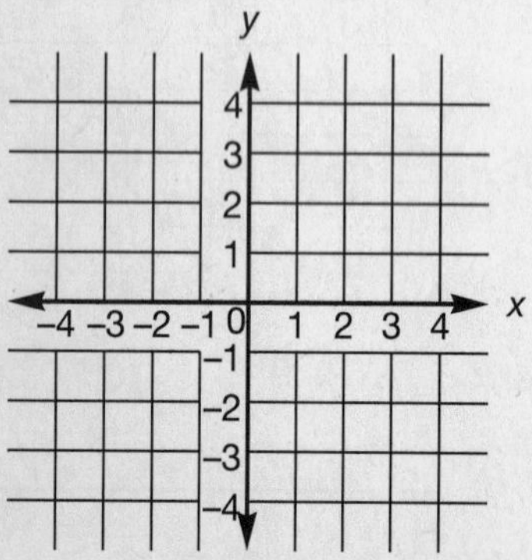

8. $y < -x + 1$

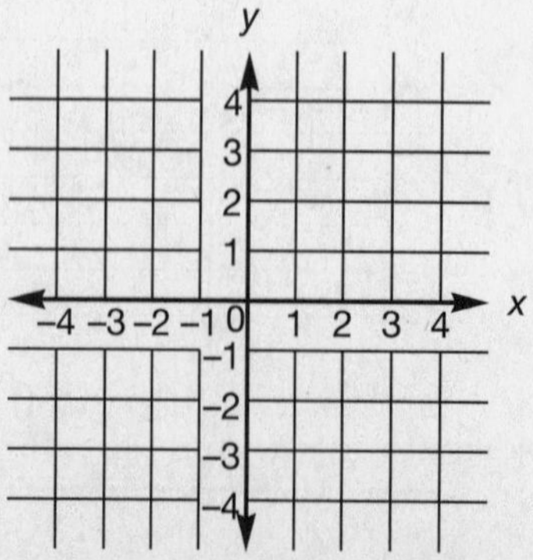

9. $x > -4$

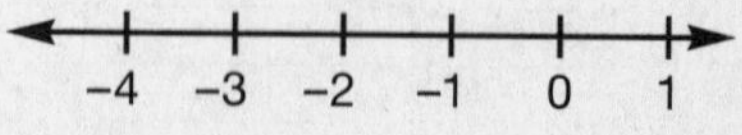

NAME

SHARPEN YOUR SKILLS

Translating Figures

Slide the figure left 14 units and up 9 units.

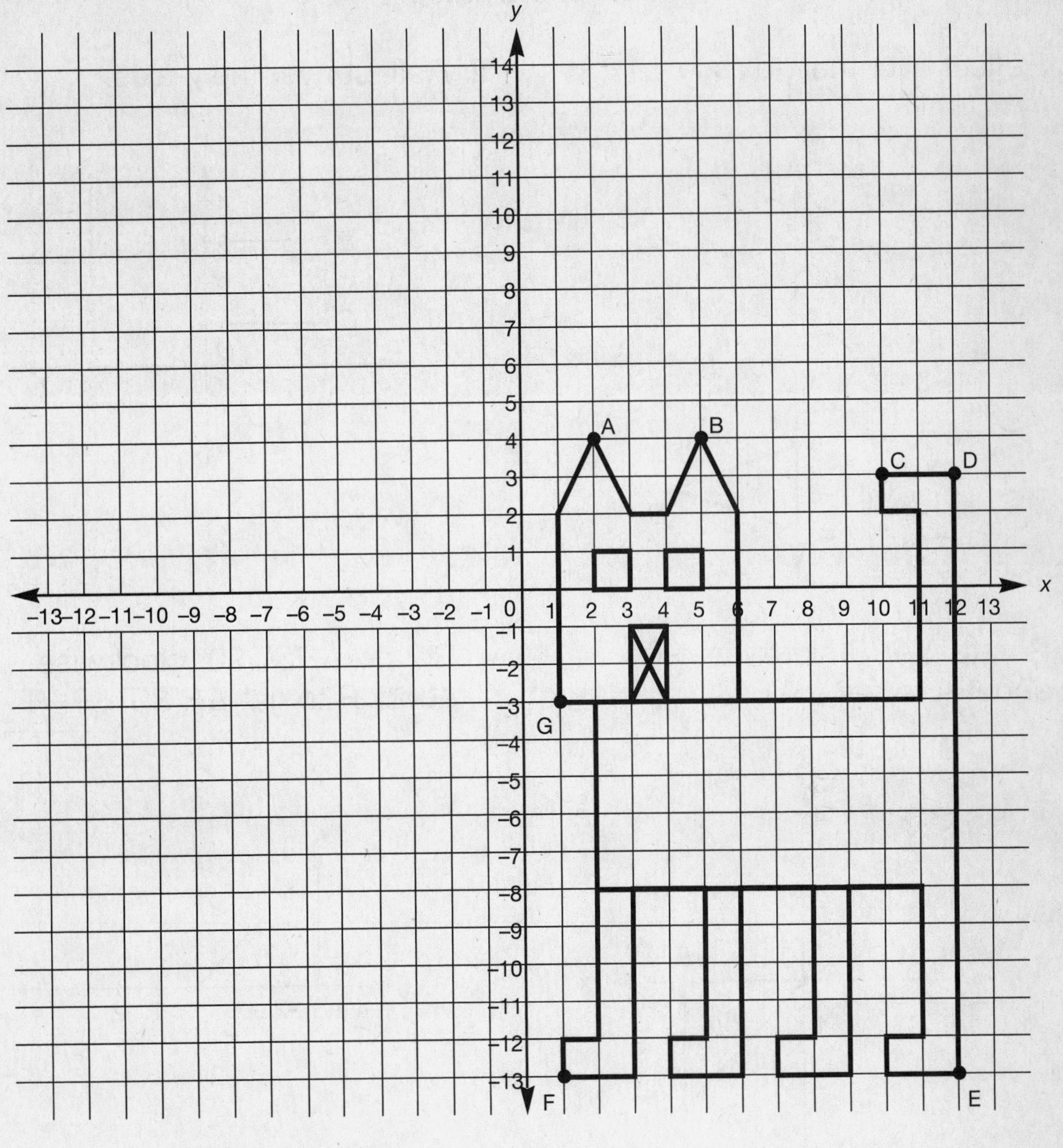

Give the coordinates of the following points.

A′ ____________ B′ ____________ C′ ____________

D′ ____________ E′ ____________ F′ ____________

G′ ____________

NAME

Reflections and Rotations

SHARPEN YOUR SKILLS

Draw the new figure on the coordinate grid. Give the original coordinates and the new coordinates.

1. Reflect over the *x*-axis.

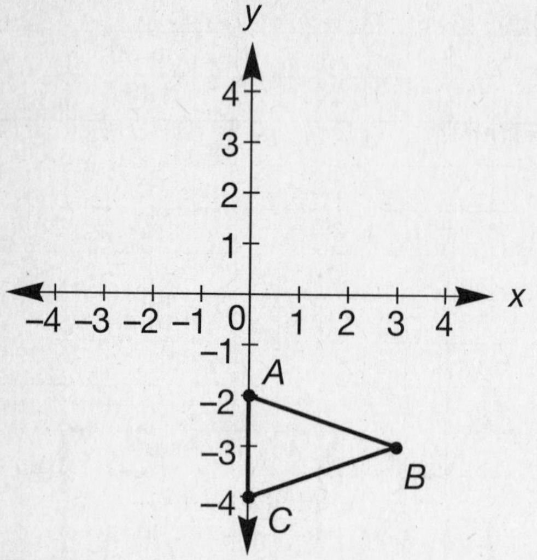

2. Reflect over the *y*-axis.

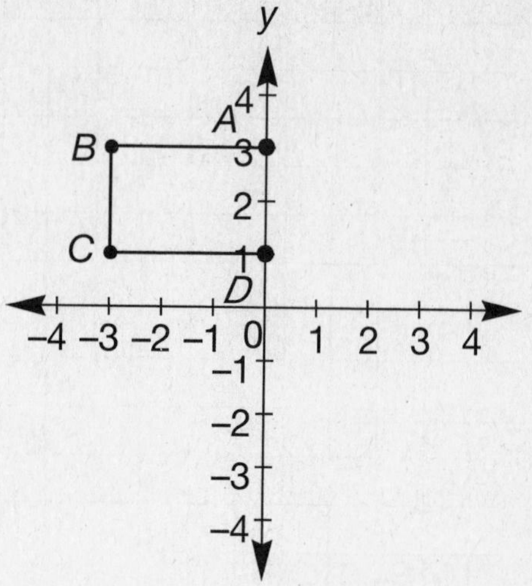

3. Rotate ΔABC clockwise 90° about *A* to get $\Delta A'B'C'$.

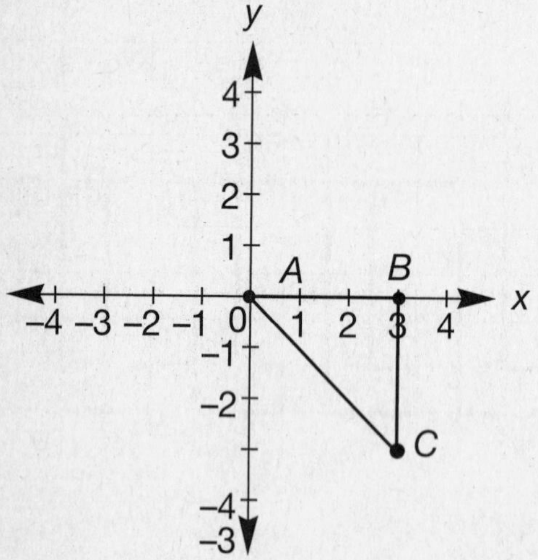

4. Rotate ΔRST 90° clockwise about *R* to get $\Delta R'S'T'$.

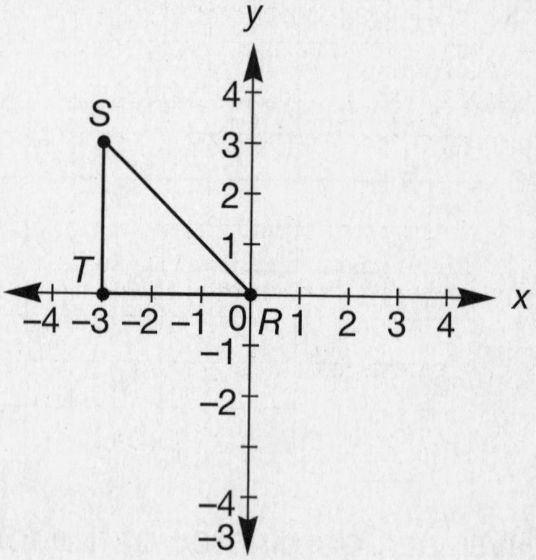

5. What happens when you rotate a figure 360°?

___

NAME

Dilations

SHARPEN YOUR SKILLS

Dilate each figure according to the indicated rule.

1. (x, y) becomes $(2x, 2y)$ **2.** (x, y) becomes $(3x, 3y)$ **3.** (x, y) becomes $(-2x, -2y)$

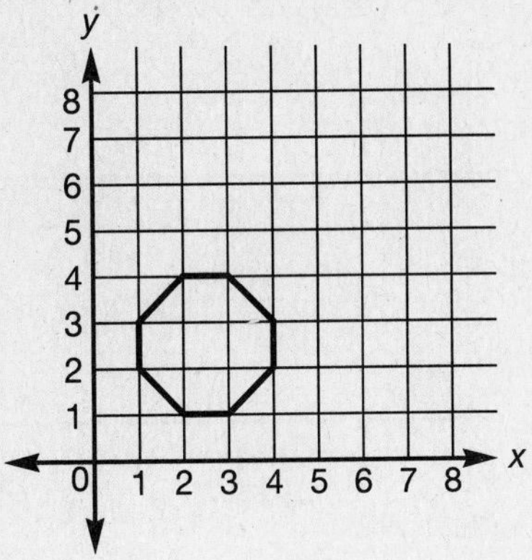

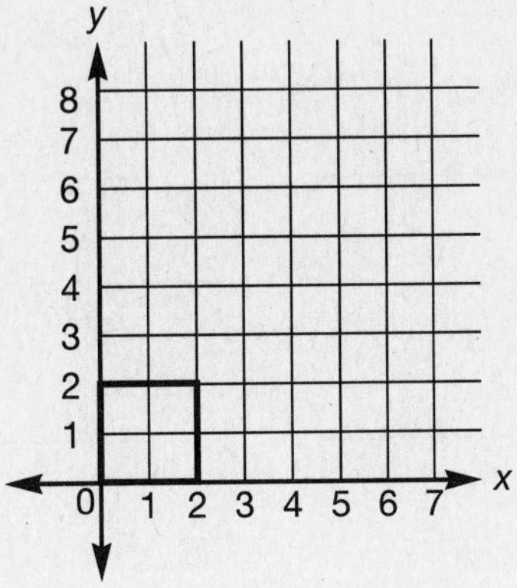

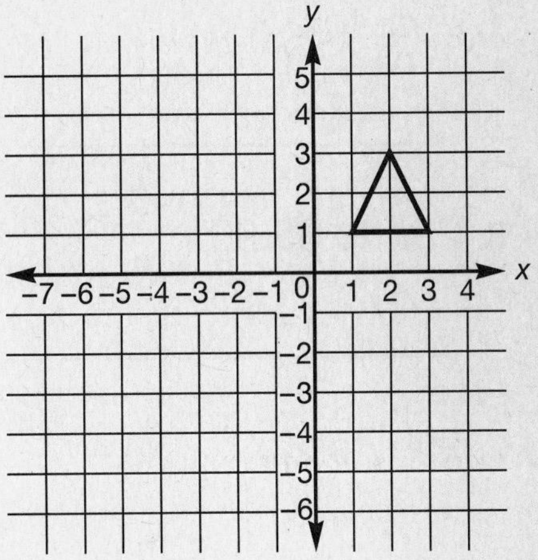

Indicate by what rule Figure A was transformed to Figure B.

4.

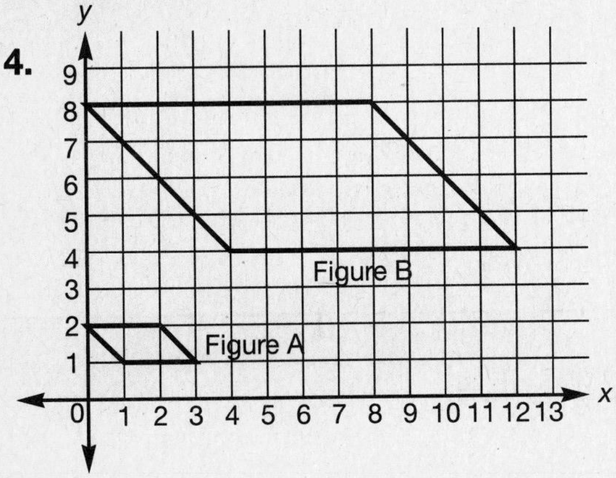

5.

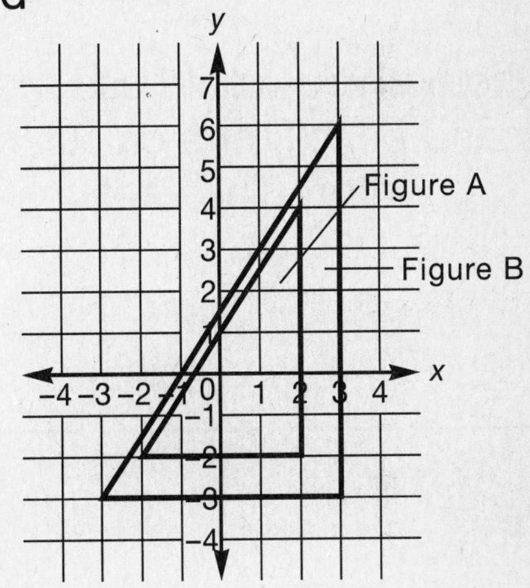

______________________ ______________________

Mixed Practice Name the quadrilateral that is a result of the transformation.

6. A translation of Figure 1

____

7. A dilation of Figure 1

____

8. A reflection of Figure 1 about the y-axis

____

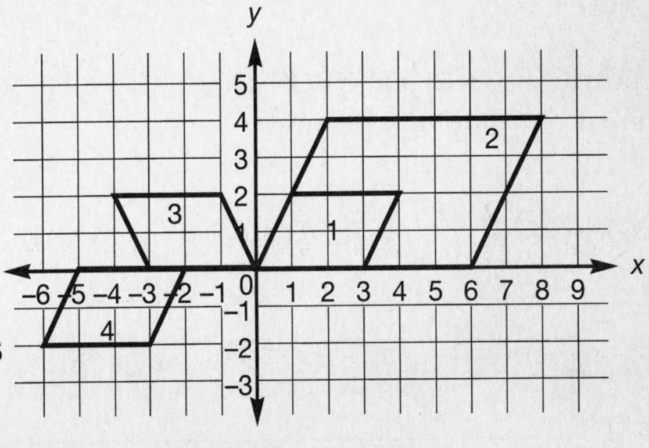

NAME

Ratio and Proportion

SHARPEN YOUR SKILLS

Rewrite the units so they are the same.
Then write a ratio in the simplest form.

1. 7 in. to 2 ft

2. 8 oz to 3 lb

3. 25¢ to $5.00

4. 5 g to 3 kg

5. 9 in. to 2 yd

6. 5 to 3 dozen

Tell whether you would use mental math, paper and pencil, or a calculator to solve each proportion. Then solve each proportion.

7. $\frac{4}{5} = \frac{b}{35}$

8. $\frac{x}{19} = \frac{84}{114}$

9. $\frac{56}{d} = \frac{7}{8}$

10. $\frac{216}{18} = \frac{504}{s}$

11. $\frac{8}{t} = \frac{2}{9}$

12. $\frac{y}{63} = \frac{3}{9}$

Write a rate for each problem. Then write the rate in simplest form.

13. 150 mi in 2.5 hours

14. $72 for 6 shirts

Use after pages 184–187.

NAME

SHARPEN YOUR SKILLS

Using Proportions to Solve Percent Problems

Solve each proportion.

1. $\frac{n}{100} = \frac{25}{5}$

   $n =$ ________

2. $\frac{12}{100} = \frac{n}{500}$

   $n =$ ________

3. $\frac{6}{n} = \frac{30}{100}$

   $n =$ ________

4. $\frac{40}{100} = \frac{24}{n}$

   $n =$ ________

5. $\frac{50}{100} = \frac{2}{n}$

   $n =$ ________

6. $\frac{9}{n} = \frac{25}{100}$

   $n =$ ________

7. $\frac{2.5}{12.5} = \frac{n}{100}$

   $n =$ ________

8. $\frac{n}{100} = \frac{8}{20}$

   $n =$ ________

9. $\frac{2.5}{100} = \frac{8.2}{n}$

   $n =$ ________

10. $\frac{1.5}{n} = \frac{7.5}{100}$

    $n =$ ________

Write a proportion and solve.

11. ____________ % of 270 is 135.

12. 144 is ____________ % of 200.

13. 27 is 90% of ____________.

14. 90% of ____________ is 18.

15. 20% of 455 is ____________.

16. ____________ is 50% of 120.

NAME

SHARPEN YOUR SKILLS

Write an Equation

Solve an equation for each problem.

1. A certain robot can weld 400 connections in 0.5 hour. How long would it take this robot to weld 3,000 connections?

____

2. Another robot can weld 300 connections in 0.45 hour. How many connections can this robot finish welding in 2 hours?

____

3. One type of robot moves 54 feet in 3 seconds. How far can this robot move in 12 seconds?

____

Each problem gives the speed of a computer printer. Find the number of seconds it would take the printer to print 2,000 lines.

4. Chain: 200 lines in 6 seconds

____

5. Matrix: 60 lines in 9 seconds

____

Each 10K of memory in a microcomputer can store 10,240 bytes of information. Find the number of bytes that can be stored in computers with the given memory.

6. 8K

____

7. 16 K

____

Use after pages 190–191.

NAME

SHARPEN YOUR SKILLS

Ratios in Geometry

Find the width of a golden rectangle with each of these given lengths.

1. 6.5 meters ________

2. 432 yards ________

3. 10.4 cm ________

4. 2.72 in. ________

Find the length of a golden rectangle with each of these given widths.

5. 3.2 centimeters ________

6. 5.7 feet ________

7. 4.8 yards ________

8. 3.5 m ________

9. 2.7 ft ________

10. 104 mm ________

Estimation Estimate the diameter of each circle.

11. $C = 44$ ________

12. $C = 4.7$ ________

13. $C = 36$ ________

14. $C = 48$ ________

NAME

SHARPEN YOUR SKILLS

Percents, Fractions, and Decimals

Complete the table. Write the fractions in lowest terms.

Fraction	Decimal	Percent	Fraction	Decimal	Percent
	0.25		$\frac{3}{5}$		
	$0.1\overline{6}$			0.575	
$\frac{1}{2}$					40%
		75%			39%
$\frac{1}{1}$	1	100%	$\frac{1}{3}$		
	0.7		$\frac{3}{10}$		
		1%			5%
$\frac{1}{5}$				0.875	
$\frac{9}{10}$			$\frac{1}{10}$		
	0.8				37.5%
$\frac{5}{6}$				0.625	
$\frac{1}{8}$			$\frac{7}{20}$		

NAME

SHARPEN YOUR SKILLS

Equations for Percent Problems

Tell whether you would use mental math, paper and pencil, or a calculator. Then solve each equation.

1. $62\% \times 90 = m$

2. $40\% \times 120 = m$

3. $100\% \times 84 = m$

4. $15\% \times 34 = m$

5. $63\frac{1}{2}\% \times 55 = m$

6. $300\% \times 40 = m$

7. $110\% \times 19 = m$

8. $65\% \times 9 = m$

Write an equation for each problem. Then solve.

9. What is 3% of 478?

10. 16 is what percent of 64?

11. Find $33\frac{1}{3}\%$ of 39.

12. What is 9% of 2,100?

13. 7.4 is what percent of 40?

14. Find 52% of 132.

Mixed Practice Write a proportion and an equation for each question.

15. 15 is what percent of 30?

16. What percent of 20 is 12.5?

NAME

SHARPEN YOUR SKILLS

Mental Math with Percents

Tell whether you would use mental math or paper and pencil. Then find each answer.

1. 50% of 120 is ________.

2. ________ of 240 is 180.

3. 25% of 160 is ________.

4. $66\frac{2}{3}$% of 1.80 is ________.

5. ________ of 120 is 30.

6. 40% of ________ is 4.

7. 20% of ________ is 10.

8. 60% of 25 is ________.

9. $33\frac{1}{3}$% of 99 is ________.

10. 30% of 300 is ________.

Solve each problem.

11. A record shop is giving a 20% discount on records normally selling for $10.00. What will one record cost?

____

12. A bicycle that sells for $120.00 is advertised as selling for $80.00. What is the percent of discount?

____

NAME

SHARPEN YOUR SKILLS

Estimating Percents

Circle the best estimate. **Remember** to use common percents and equivalent fractions or decimals.

1. 24.8% of the voters voted no.

About $\frac{1}{3}$ of the voters voted no.

About $\frac{1}{4}$ of the voters voted no.

About 1 out of 2 voted no.

2. 12% of the students got an A.

About 12 students got an A.

About $\frac{1}{2}$ of the students got an A.

About 1 out of 10 students got an A.

Solve using estimation.

3. 1,200 long distance calls were made by the Alamo Iron Works employees. 34% were made in July. About how many calls were made in July? ____________

4. John has 180 coins in his collection. Approximately 67% of the coins are dimes. About how many dimes does he have?

____

5. Classes at McCullough Middle School are 60 minutes each. Approximately how many minutes are spent on each activity?

Introducing new topics	24%	______
Review	20%	______
Guided Practice	32%	______
Discussion	10%	______
Other	14%	______

6. Kristen got an 80 on her Spanish test. There were 20 problems in all. How many were correct?

____

Use after pages 202–203.

NAME

Solving Percent Problems

SHARPEN YOUR SKILLS

Write an equation and solve it to determine the number of people attending each sporting event.

Attendance at School Sporting Events
15,000 Fans

Basketball	35%
Football	30%
Baseball	20%
Soccer	15%

1. Basketball ______________________

____

2. Football ______________________

____

3. Baseball ______________________

____

4. Soccer ______________________

____

Write an equation and solve it to show the percent of students who chose each of the following activities.

Favorite School Activities
14,000 Students

Sports	4,900
Music	3,500
Drama	2,800
Art	700
Other	2,100

5. Sports ______________________

____

6. Music ______________________

____

Write an equation and solve it to find the total number of students working at each job.

Percentage of Students with Part-Time Jobs

Babysitting	35%
Newspaper delivery	40%
Store clerk	10%
Other	15%

7. If there are 4,200 students, how many babysit?

____

____

8. If there are 5,400 students, how many have newspaper routes?

____

____

NAME

SHARPEN YOUR SKILLS

Write an Equation

Write and solve an equation. If necessary, round to the nearest cent.

1. Levi bought a stereo system on sale for $264. The original price was $330. What percent of the original price did he pay?

2. Ana bought a record-cleaning kit that was reduced by 10% from its original price of $5.50. How much money did she save?

3. Pat bought a pocket-size calculator for $9.98. This was 85% of the original price. What was the original price of the calculator?

4. Joan paid $16.59 for an FM booster that originally cost $19.75. What percent of the original price did she pay?

5. Ariel paid $33\frac{1}{3}$% down for a set of earphones that costs $84. How much was her down payment?

6. An item sold for $1.47. The tax on it was 6%. How much was the tax?

7. A smoke alarm was on sale at a discount of $2.49 from its original cost of $21.99. The discount was what percent of the original cost?

IS YOUR ANSWER REASONABLE?

NAME

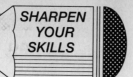

Income and Commissions

SHARPEN YOUR SKILLS

The table gives information on the earnings of the employees of the Hap-Along-Shoe store. Find each person's gross income to the nearest cent.

Name	Total Sales	Commission Rate	Weekly Salary	Gross Pay
1. Bob Pedal	$1,357.00	2.5%	$265	______
2. Ann Footworthy	$1,721.00	3%	$315	______
3. Lyn Sole	$1,216.00	1%	$250	______
4. Larry Brogan	$1,258.00	2%	$260	______

Mixed Practice Complete the following.

5. 7% of $250 is ______.

6. 6% of ______ is $27.00.

Solve each problem. **Remember** to check your work.

7. 28% of Whitney's gross income is deducted. What is her net income if her gross income is $1,250?

______

8. Bonita earns a weekly salary of $275 selling cosmetics. She receives a 3% commission for all sales above $500. Her sales total for the week was $600. Find her gross pay.

______

9. From Bonita's gross pay, $33.36 is deducted for income tax. What percent of her gross pay is taken for income tax?

______

10. Eight percent of Bonita's gross pay is deducted for social security. How much does she pay for social security?

______

11. What is Bonita's net pay? ______

NAME

SHARPEN YOUR SKILLS

Budgets and Circle Graphs

This table shows how Vanette budgets her monthly net income. Complete the table and make a circle graph of the data. Round to the nearest degree.

Item	Percent	Degrees
Rent	$33\frac{1}{3}\%$	**1.** ______
Utilities	$12\frac{1}{2}\%$	**2.** ______
Insurance	$4\frac{1}{5}\%$	**3.** ______
Food	5%	**4.** ______
Entertainment	$3\frac{1}{3}\%$	**5.** ______
Car	$12\frac{1}{2}\%$	**6.** ______
Clothing	$5\frac{1}{5}\%$	**7.** ______
Misc./Savings	$23\frac{1}{3}\%$	**8.** ______

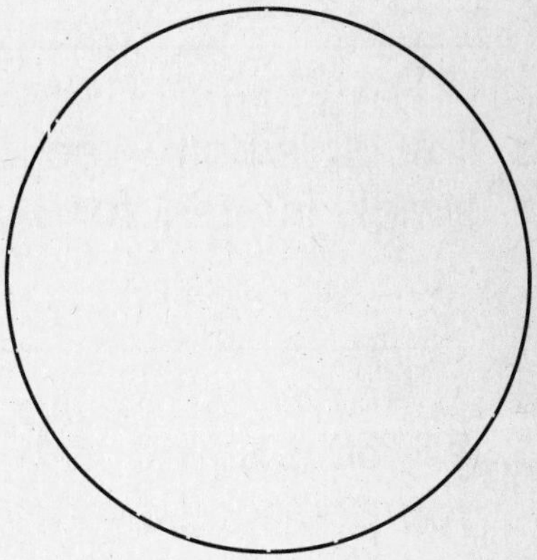

Gaston is the treasurer of the Library Club. This year he collected $600 in dues from the members. The circle graph shows how the budget was divided. Write the letter of the circle section representing each of the categories.

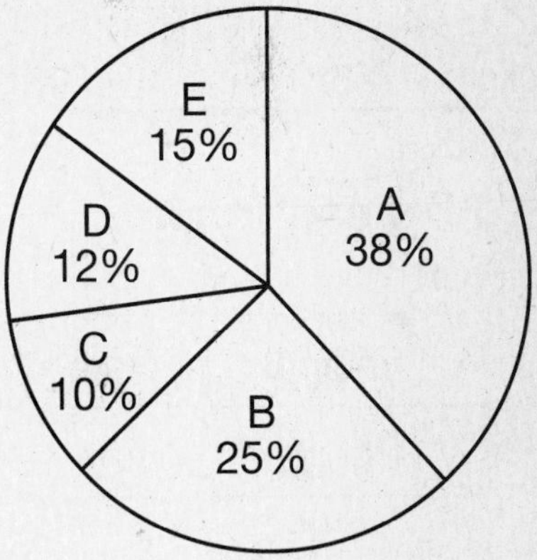

9. Guest speakers—$228.00 _____

10. Utility fee—$72.00 _____

11. Refreshments—$150.00 _____

12. Miscellaneous—$60.00 _____

13. Purchase of new books for the library—$90.00 _____

The table shows the inventory of a record store. How many degrees on a circle graph would each category require?

Category	Percent	Degrees
CDs	30%	**14.** ______
Cassettes	50%	**15.** ______
LPs	20%	**16.** ______

NAME

SHARPEN YOUR SKILLS

Use a Formula

Use the formula: Interest = (Principal)(Rate)(Time) to find the interest

1. if $400 is borrowed at 3% simple interest for 4 months.

2. if $4,500 is borrowed at 9.5% simple interest for 6 months.

3. if $800 is borrowed at 5.75% simple interest for 3 years.

4. if $500 is saved at 8% interest compounded annually for 3 years.

5. if $750 is saved at 10% interest compounded annually for 5 years.

Find the total amount in the account

6. if $3,500 is invested at 12.5% simple interest for 4 years.

7. if $5,000 is invested at 20% simple interest for 3 months.

8. Find each answer. Use the simple-interest formula.

Principal	Rate	Time	Interest
$3,000	8%		$480
	12%	$1\frac{1}{2}$ years	$60
$900		2 years	$135
	9.2%	5 years	$322
$900		2 years	$288

NAME

Comparison Shopping

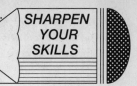

SHARPEN YOUR SKILLS

Find the unit price of each item to the nearest tenth of a cent.

1. a 16-oz package of crab meat for $2.05 ____
2. a 24-oz container of cottage cheese for $1.10 ____
3. an 8-oz can of hairspray for $2.00 ____
4. 5 bagels for a dollar ____
5. a 24-exposure roll of film for $2.79 ____

The table shows the items on Johannah's shopping list. Find the unit price to the nearest tenth of a cent. Then, find the difference in price between the brand name product and the generic item.

Item	Name Brand	Unit Cost	Generic	Unit Cost	Difference
Paper Towels	59¢ for 75 sheets	**6.**	42¢ for 75	**7.**	**8.**
Popcorn	$1.09 for 2 lb	**9.**	72¢ for 2 lb	**10.**	**11.**
Beans	78¢ for 16 oz	**12.**	44¢ for 16 oz	**13.**	**14.**
Macaroni	$1.19 for 24 oz	**15.**	$1.02 for 32 oz	**16.**	**17.**
Light bulbs	$1.89 for 4	**18.**	79¢ for 2	**19.**	**20.**
Hair spray	$1.49 for 7 oz	**21.**	89¢ for 7 oz	**22.**	**23.**

24. Reggie must decide between two pairs of running shoes. Pair A costs $59.99, and pair B costs $65.00. Give some factors, other than price, that may affect his decision.

____

____

NAME

Multiple-Step Problems

SHARPEN YOUR SKILLS

Solve each problem.

1. A washing machine that lists for $620 is on sale for 15% off the list price. Find the sale price.

____

2. A $52.50 screen door is on sale for $42. Find the percent of discount on the door.

____

3. A mini-bike costs $414 plus 6.5% sales tax. What is the total cost of the bike?

____

4. A suede jacket costs $247 plus 8% sales tax. What is the cost of the jacket?

____

5. A $15 sweatshirt went on sale for 6% off. Later, the sale price was discounted by 10%. What was the new sale price?

____

6. A $146 tent was sold for 20% off. There was a sales tax of 4%. What was the total cost of the tent?

____

Copy the table and fill in the missing values.
Hint: First round the sale price to the nearest dollar.

Item	Regular price	Rate of discount	Amount of discount	Rounded sale price	Sale price
Microwave	$600.00	**7.**	**8.**	**9.**	$389.50
Television	$560.00	**10.**	**11.**	**12.**	$251.99
Stereo	$375.00	**13.**	**14.**	**15.**	$149.95

NAME

SHARPEN YOUR SKILLS

Interpreting Utility Bills

Fill in the missing numbers in the bill for electricity. Use a calculator or pencil and paper and round each number to the nearest cent.

Present meter reading	August 9		88679
Previous meter reading	July 11		86829
Total kwh used			**1.** ______
Customer charge			$3.00
Energy charge 1st 400 kwh		× 0.0810	**2.** ______
Remaining kwh	**3.** ______	× 0.0397	**4.** ______
State tax	**5.** ______	× 0.00340	**6.** ______
Amount due			**7.** ______

Use the utility statement to answer each problem.

SERVICE ADDR.

ACCT. #

SAN. UNITS 0

WTR. MTR. SIZE 5/8

KWH CONSTANT 1

SERVICE	01/09 READ	12/07 READ	CONSUMPTION	CHARGE	SERVICE	CHARGE
ELC	ELECTRIC	CUSTOMER	CHARGE	300	GAR	825
E01	72219	72045	174	479	T03	64
ELF	.012380		174	215	DRR	130
SUB-TOTAL ELECTRIC - - - - -				984	ALR	115
T02				10		
W01	2417	2395	22	591		
WW1			22	633		
					CUR	3362
					PRB	3402
					TOTAL	$67.64
					PENALTY	$1.12
						$68.76
						10/09/89

FOR ASSISTANCE CALL ➡ 555-2778

$68.76 ⬅ PAY THIS AMOUNT AFTER DUE DATE

10/09/89 ⬅ DUE DATE

CITY OF AUSTIN UTILITY STATEMENT

OFFICES (open Monday through Friday)

TDD for Hearing Impaired. 555-3663.

The City is complying with Section 504 of the 1973 Rehabilitation Act.

Water is billed in 100s of gallons.

YOUR PAYMENT FOR THE TOTAL MUST BE RECEIVED IN THIS OFFICE ON/BEFORE DUE DATE OR A PENALTY IS CHARGED.

8. If the customer is hearing impaired, what telephone number can be dialed for assistance?

____

9. In what quantity is water billed?

____

10. What days are the utility offices open? ______________________

11. What is the due date of this bill?

____

NAME

SHARPEN YOUR SKILLS

Using Credit Cards

Solve each problem.

1. If the annual interest rate for a credit card is 19%, what is the monthly interest rate?

____

2. If the annual interest rate for a credit card is 19%, and this month's unpaid balance is $300.90, how much will the customer pay in interest this month?

____

Complete the table. Round the interest to the nearest cent. Use pencil and paper or a calculator.

Unpaid Balance	Payment	Balance after payment	Interest rate (per month)	Amount of Interest	New Purchase	New Balance
$54.54	$20	**3.**	1.25%	**4.**	$35.60	**5.**
$34.80	$0	**6.**	1.25%	**7.**	$16.00	**8.**
$78.98	$25	**9.**	1.5%	**10.**	$13.98	**11.**
$215.98	$50	**12.**	1.5%	**13.**	$72.44	**14.**
$463.42	$65	**15.**	1.5%	**16.**	$44.88	**17.**

18. Last month the Bundys' unpaid balance on a credit card was $57.88. They made a $35.00 payment and charged purchases of $19.99, $27.88, and $17.49. If the card's annual interest rate is 18%, what is this month's unpaid balance?

____

NAME

SHARPEN YOUR SKILLS

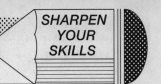

Installment Buying

Find the cost of financing and the annual rate of interest being charged. Round the rate of interest to the nearest tenth.

Item	List price	Number of payments	Amount of each payment	Cost of financing	Annual rate of interest
VCR	$350	12	$32.65	**1.**	**2.**
Cassette player	$225	12	$22.13	**3.**	**4.**
Compact disc player	$439	18	$29.84	**5.**	**6.**
Computer	$1,750	24	$81.17	**7.**	**8.**
New automobile	$21,500	60	$519.58	**9.**	**10.**
Refrigerator	$899	36	$30.07	**11.**	**12.**
Camcorder	$999	36	$49.17	**13.**	**14.**
Sailboat	$12,500	48	$313.06	**15.**	**16.**

Solve each problem.

17. The Bryants bought a used van for $24,500, including tax. They paid 20% down and the balance in 60 payments of $356.06. What was the total cost of the van?

____

18. How much was the down payment?

____

19. How much interest did they pay?

____

NAME

Multiple-Step Problems

SHARPEN YOUR SKILLS

Find the percent of increase or decrease to the nearest tenth of a percent.

1. 80 to 98 ____________

2. 35 to 66 ____________

3. 41 to 27 ____________

4. 17 to 44 ____________

5. 7 to 11 ____________

6. 42 to 21 ____________

7. 24 to 25 ____________

8. 10 to 3 ____________

9. 27 to 31 ____________

10. 33 to 62 ____________

11. 98 to 109 ____________

12. 28 to 13 ____________

Find the amount of increase or decrease and the new amount.

13. 16 with a 16% increase

____

14. 129 with a 4% decrease

____

15. 100 with a 52% decrease

____

16. 23 with a 6% decrease

____

17. 8 with a 10% increase

____

18. 56 with a 22% increase

____

19. 79 with an 8% decrease

____

20. 30 with a 43% increase

____

NAME

SHARPEN YOUR SKILLS

Interpreting Data from a Graph

Ms. Kolcznk keeps the attendance records at a high school. Here is a graph of the data for a three-week period during a flu epidemic.

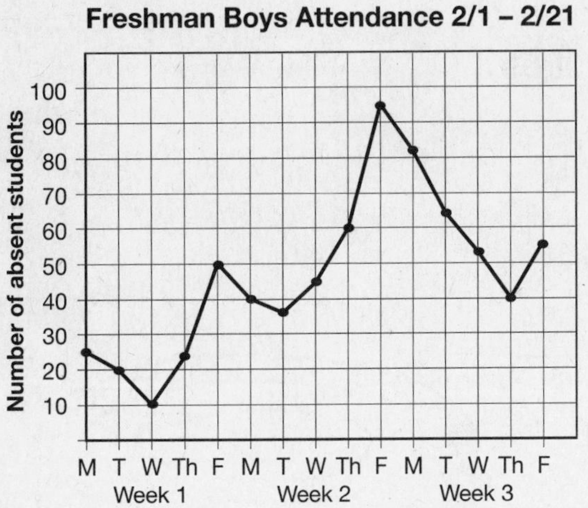

1. On what day was absenteeism highest during Week 1?

____

2. On what day was it lowest during Week 2?

____

3. During what week was the overall absenteeism greatest?

____

The Peculiar Pie Company tested its new pie flavor, ketchup pie, against its old standard, persimmon pie. One hundred males and 100 females in each age group were tested.

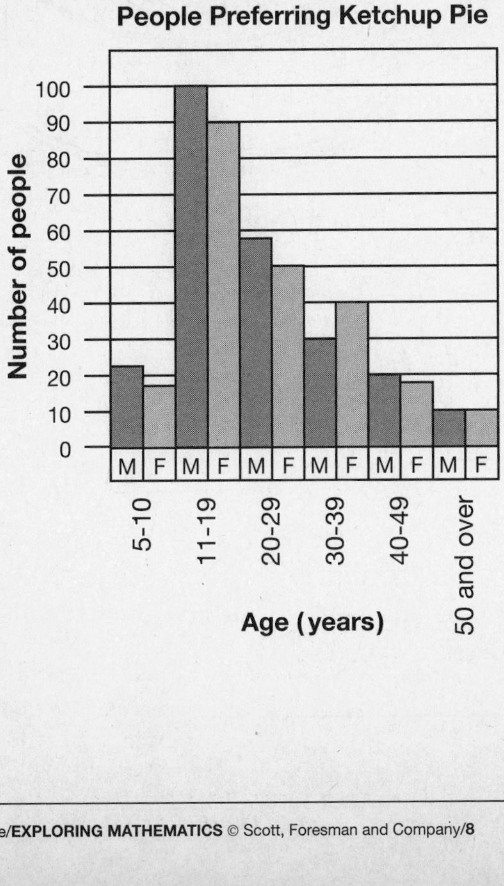

4. How many men in the 40–49 group preferred the ketchup pie?

____

5. The ketchup pie was most popular among what age group?

____

6. How many women in the 20–29 age group preferred persimmon pie?

____

Use after pages 238–241.

NAME

SHARPEN YOUR SKILLS

Deciding When an Estimate Is Enough

Solve. Use mental math, paper and pencil, or a calculator. Tell which method you used.

1. The Brack Brick Company is providing bricks for a new building. Each wall requires 1,670 bricks per story. The building is octagonal in shape and 12 stories high. Estimate the number of bricks that the Brack Brick Company will need to provide.

____

2. The sub shop serves one fourth of a dill pickle with each of its sandwiches. The pickles are ordered in containers of whole pickles which contain about 15 pickles. If the sub shop sells an average of 350 sandwiches per week, how many containers of pickles will need to be ordered?

____

3. Mr. Cuisine requires the students in his literature classes to read *Wurst and Pizza.* The book is 1,080 pages long. Mattie wants to estimate the number of words in the book. She counts 33 lines on a typical page. She counts 11 words on a typical line. Estimate how many words she will be reading.

____

4. Cornelia cans corn. Each can of Cornelia's corn contains about 2 cups of corn. How many quarts of corn will Cornelia can in 756 cans of corn (4 cups per quart)?

____

NAME ______

Customary Units of Measurement

SHARPEN YOUR SKILLS

Number Sense Choose the best answer.

1. Weight of a book

1 oz   100 oz   1 lb

2. Weight of a car

2,000 oz   2,000 lb   2,000 ton

3. Width of a tennis court

4 ft   40 ft   140 ft

4. Volume of a suitcase

6 cu in.   6 cu ft   6 cu yd

Find each missing number.

5. 18 c = ______ pt

6. 35 oz = ______ lb ______ oz

7. 8 yd = ______ ft

8. 7 lb 5 oz = ______ oz

9. $3\frac{1}{2}$ ft = ______ yd

10. 16 fl oz = ______ c

11. 99 qt = ______ gal ______ qt

12. 12 qt 2 pt = ______ pt

13. 144 oz = ______ lb

14. $\frac{1}{4}$ mi = ________ ft

15. $\frac{1}{2}$ cu yd = _______ cu ft

16. $\frac{3}{4}$ sq ft = ______ sq in.

17. 7 cu ft = ______ cu yd

18. 72 qt = ______ gal

19. 8,000 lb = ______ ton

20. 6 qt = ______ gal ______ qt

21. 15 gal = ______ qt

22. 1,400 lb = ______ ton

Solve each problem.

23. An order of groceries weighed 17 lb 12 oz. How many ounces is this?

____

24. Jason needs 9 yd of wire. If it is sold in packages of 72 in., how many packages should he buy?

____

Use after pages 258–261.

NAME

SHARPEN YOUR SKILLS

Computing with Customary Measures

Add or subtract. **Remember,** you may have to regroup.

1. 12 ft 7 in. + 9 ft 2 in.

2. 12 lb 9 oz + 26 lb 6 oz

3. 8 qt 5 pt − 2 qt 2 pt

4. 15 lb − 4 lb 9 oz

5. 5 yd 2 ft + 10 yd 2 ft

6. 12 gal 2 qt − 3 gal 3 qt

7. 12 lb − 11 oz

8. 15 ft − 3 ft 9 in.

9. 32 ft 5 in. + 19 ft 7 in.

10. 6 yd 2 ft 9 in. + 2 yd 11 in. = ________

Solve each problem.

Dan is helping a group of children build a snow fort.

11. Each of the walls is to be 4 ft high. If the walls are 2 ft 9 in. high, how much remains to be added to each?

____

12. Each of the 4 walls is 6 ft long. What is the total distance around the fort?

____

Arrange the amounts in order from least to greatest.

13. $2\frac{3}{4}$ ft   1 yd   72 in.

____

14. 15 fl oz   1 pt $1\frac{1}{2}$ c

____

NAME

SHARPEN YOUR SKILLS

Metric Units of Length, Area, and Volume

Find the missing number.

1. 6.4 m = ________ cm

2. 839 m^3 = ________ dam^3

3. 524 m = ________ hm

4. 36,000 m^3 = ________ hm^3

5. 346 cm = ________ m

6. 1,723 mm^3 = ________ cm^3

7. 86 m = ________ dm

8. 0.036 cm = ________ mm

9. 32 dam = ________ m

10. 428 dam = ________ m

11. 0.4 m = ________ cm

12. 496 mm = ________ cm

13. 8,241 mm = ________ m

14. 183.4 cm = ________ m

15. 6,340 m = ________ km

16. 14 m^3 = ________ dm^3

17. 628 mm^3 = ________ cm^3

18. 983 mm^3 = ________ cm^3

Solve the problem.

19. A bridge is 2.04 km long and 0.467 km wide. Express its dimensions in meters.

____

____

Mixed Practice Complete.

20. 4 yd 2 ft = ☐ ft

21. 18 qt = ☐ gal ☐ qt

22. 781 mm = ☐ m

23. 15 yd = ☐ ft

24. 20 oz = ☐ lb ☐ oz

25. 4 cm^2 = ☐ mm^2

NAME

SHARPEN YOUR SKILLS

Metric Units of Capacity and Mass

Find the missing number.

1. 812 mg = ______________ g

2. 25 L = ______________ cL

3. 420 mL = ______________ L

4. 652 g = ______________ kg

5. 26 dag = ______________ dg

6. 863 kg = ______________ g

Estimation Choose the best measure. **Remember** to look at the units.

7. Mass of a pencil

1.93 g 19.3 g 193 g

8. Mass of a bowling ball

0.5 kg 5 kg 50 kg

9. Mass of a large dog

0.4 kg 4 kg 40 kg

10. Mass of a paper clip

5 mg 50 mg 500 mg

Shade in a path so that the amounts in the boxes in your path are in order from smallest to largest. The path may go through all but two boxes before you arrive at the end. Shorter paths are also possible.

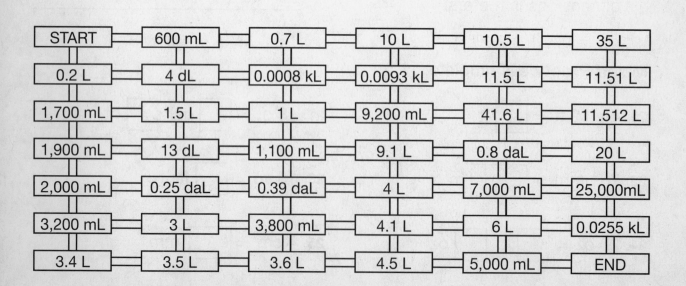

START	600 mL	0.7 L	10 L	10.5 L	35 L
0.2 L	4 dL	0.0008 kL	0.0093 kL	11.5 L	11.51 L
1,700 mL	1.5 L	1 L	9,200 mL	41.6 L	11.512 L
1,900 mL	13 dL	1,100 mL	9.1 L	0.8 daL	20 L
2,000 mL	0.25 daL	0.39 daL	4 L	7,000 mL	25,000mL
3,200 mL	3 L	3,800 mL	4.1 L	6 L	0.0255 kL
3.4 L	3.5 L	3.6 L	4.5 L	5,000 mL	END

NAME

SHARPEN YOUR SKILLS

Computing With Metric Measures

Compute.

1. 5 m + 12 m + 4 m ________
2. 3,245 cm − 1,987 cm ________
3. 3.45 kg − 0.78 kg ________

4. 80 mm = ________ cm
5. 946 mL = ________ L
6. 0.79 g = ________ kg
7. 2,850 mg = ________ g
8. 7.7 cm = ________ mm
9. 6,300 L = ________ kL
10. 5.35 m ÷ 0.05 = ________ m
11. 0.3246 kg ÷ 30 = ________ kg

Compute. **Remember** to use square and cubic units where necessary.

12. 48.6 kL − 1,350 L = ________ L
13. 275 m − 780 cm = ________ m
14. 73.2 L + 18 mL = ________ L
15. 7.5 cm × 1.7 cm = ________ cm^2
16. 36.7 kg − 171 g = ________ kg
17. 15,000 mg + 7.2 g = ________ mg
18. 6,124 mg ÷ 400 = ________ mg
19. 12 cm × 32 cm × 50 cm = ________ cm^3
20. On a map 1 cm represents 250 km. If two cities are 4 cm apart on the map, find the actual distance between the two cities.

____

Use after pages 268–269.

NAME

Give Sensible Answers

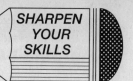

SHARPEN YOUR SKILLS

Choose the most sensible answer for each blank.
Use the following list.

120 cm   10 m $10,000   4 m   3,000 kg   50 m^2

250 m^3 10,000 m^2 10 L $3,750   555-T-U-S-K

Exclusive in the *Harrington Times,* N.Y., May 5

The circus came to town today. An elephant moved an animal cage, a spacious size of ________, and then strolled away before being stopped by his trainers. He side-stepped into a tent ________ high. The tent was badly torn and collapsed. The trainers led him off and roped him to a post. Then he drank ________ of water. While drinking, he stepped into a smaller pail and knocked over the ________ high post holding his rope. Then he scooped up Mr. Irving Flat, a bystander, lifting him ________ above the ground. The workers were able to divert the elephant away from an area of ________, covered by the largest tent, to an area of ________ where he released Mr. Flat unharmed. The elephant, said to be a small one at ________, was blamed for damages up to ________ by one spokesperson. However, another spokesperson gave a lower estimate of ________. If you wish to see the circus, call this special number for tickets: ____________________.

NAME

Number Sense in Measurement

SHARPEN YOUR SKILLS

Estimate each measurement in the appropriate metric unit.

1. 14 lb ____
2. 7 qt ____
3. 25 in. ____
4. 12 mi ____

Estimate each measurement in the appropriate customary unit.

5. 7.4 km ____
6. 5 m ____
7. 14 cm ____
8. 7 L ____

Arrange in order from least to greatest.

9. 15 in., 25 cm, length of a pencil

10. 120 oz, 3 kg, 5-lb bag of flour

Estimate. Use mental math to find the answers.

11. Mandy plans to visit her grandmother this summer. If she travels 328 km, about how many miles will she travel?

12. At the supermarket Mrs. Swift purchased an 8-ounce package of cheese. About how many kilograms did she buy?

13. During practice Matt must swim 15 laps of the pool, a lap being 2 lengths. The pool is 50 meters long. About how many yards does he swim?

14. About how many gallons are there in four 3-liter bottles of soda?

NAME

Use Data from a Table

SHARPEN YOUR SKILLS

Train Schedule

Train Number	95	171	161	173	175
Days of Operation	Daily	Ex Su	Su only	Daily	Daily
Boston, MA (ET) Dp	7:30A	8:25A	8:25A	10:15A	12:30P
New Haven, CT Ar	10:08A	11:03A	11:05A	12:57P	3:05P
New Haven, CT Dp	10:25A	11:21A	11:24A	1:15P	3:23P
New York, NY Ar	12:04P	12:57P	1:00P	2:58P	5:05P

Solve. Use the information from the table.

1. Jessica is planning a trip from Boston to New Haven. She must arrive in New Haven for an 11 A.M. meeting. Which train must she take?

   ____

   How long will the trip take?

   ____

2. How many minutes from her time of arrival will Jessica have to get to her meeting if her train arrives at the expected time?

   ____

3. Will must travel from New Haven to New York on Sunday. Which train should he take if he wants to arrive before 1:00 P.M.?

   ____

4. What is the latest Neal can depart if he plans to travel from New Haven to New York on Sunday?

   ____

   By which train?

   ____

5. Which train takes longer on a trip from Boston to New York, 173 or 175?

   ____

6. Which train gets you from Boston to New York in shortest time?

   ____

NAME

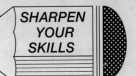

SHARPEN YOUR SKILLS

Precision and the Greatest Possible Error

Give the GPE.

1. 7 qt ______

2. $5\frac{7}{8}$ oz ______

3. 6 lb ______

4. $9\frac{2}{3}$ ft ______

5. $6\frac{5}{6}$ in. ______

6. $8\frac{7}{10}$ yd ______

7. 7.8 m ______

8. 6.62 km ______

9. 63 mg ______

10. 4.44 cm ______

11. 9.2 mL ______

12. 29 g ______

Choose the more precise unit of measure.

13. 5 L   16 mL

14. 2.6 L   23.62 L

15. 33.4 cm   16 cm

16. 14 g   15 kg

17. 8.88 kg   5.21 g

18. 8.1 L   3.2 mL

19. 212 km   14 m

20. 1.28 mL   8 mL

21. 19 m   32 km

NAME

SHARPEN YOUR SKILLS

Relative Error and Accuracy

Compute the percent error for each measurement. Then tell which measurement in each pair is more accurate.

1. 20 grams or 200 kilograms

2. $7\frac{1}{2}$ feet or 900 inches

3. 23.8 meters or 2.38 meters

For each measurement, give the GPE and the percent error to the nearest 0.1%. You may want to use a calculator.

4. 75 mi

5. 39.6 cm

6. 0.21 in.

7. 54.1 kg

8. 17.8 km

9. $1\frac{3}{4}$ yd

10. 35 oz

11. 3.03 lb

12. $24\frac{1}{8}$ in.

13. 0.774 m

14. 125 ft

15. $15\frac{1}{2}$ mi

16. 32.8° F

17. 12 min 45 sec

18. 0.8 g

19. 1.75 oz

Solve the problem.

20. Measure the length of a pencil and the length of a math textbook to the nearest inch. Calculate the percent error of each measurement. Which measurement is more accurate?

Use after pages 280–281.

NAME

SHARPEN YOUR SKILLS

Significant Digits

Complete the following table.

Measurement	Unit	Number of Units	Number of Significant Digits	Significant Digits
$72\underline{0}$ m	1 meter	720	3	**1.**
7.25 m	0.01 m	725	**2.**	**3.**
3,500 g	100 grams	**4.**	**5.**	**6.**
5,030 in.	**7.**	**8.**	**9.**	**10.**

Give the significant digits in each.

11. 4.05 lb ______

12. $6\underline{0}0$ yd ______

13. 2,334 mm ______

14. 3,100 cm ______

15. 7.4×10^3 m ______

16. 0.032 km ______

17. $7{,}9\underline{00}$ m ______

18. 2.305 mm ______

19. 3.02 g ______

20. 123.50 km ______

21. 0.02 m ______

22. 50.9 yd ______

Solve each problem.

23. Mr. Chapman measured the length of his house to be 27.4 m. How many significant digits did he use? What is the relative error?

______

24. His son had measured the length to be 27.43 m. What unit did his son use? What was the relative error?

______

25. Is the measurement of Mr. Chapman or his son more accurate? ______

26. Whose measurement is more precise? ______

NAME

SHARPEN YOUR SKILLS

Relating Planes, Lines, and Points

Name the geometric figure suggested by each picture.

1. 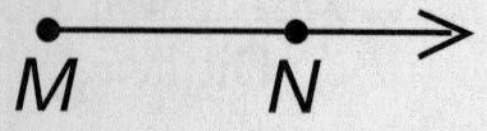

2. 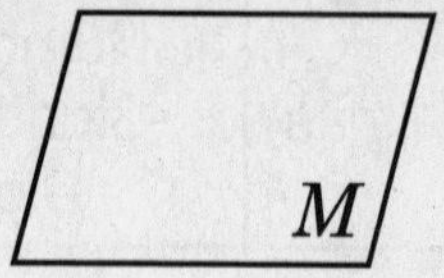

3. 

4. 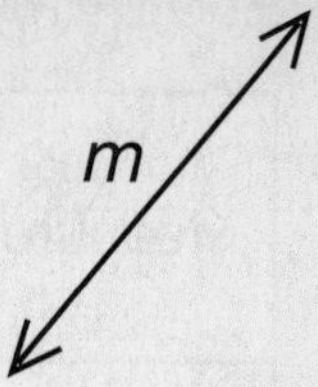

For each of Exercises 5–7, make a sketch.

5. $\overrightarrow{MS}$

6. $\overleftrightarrow{CD}$

7. $\overline{OP}$

Answer *true* or *false*.

8. Two points on the same plane are coplanar. ________

9. A point has two dimensions — length and width. ________

10. A half-line and a ray are two names for the same thing. ________

11. A plane has two dimensions — length and width. ________

12. Two points are collinear and coplanar. ________

13. Two lines on different planes cannot intersect. ________

Find each answer.

14. Name all the segments shown.

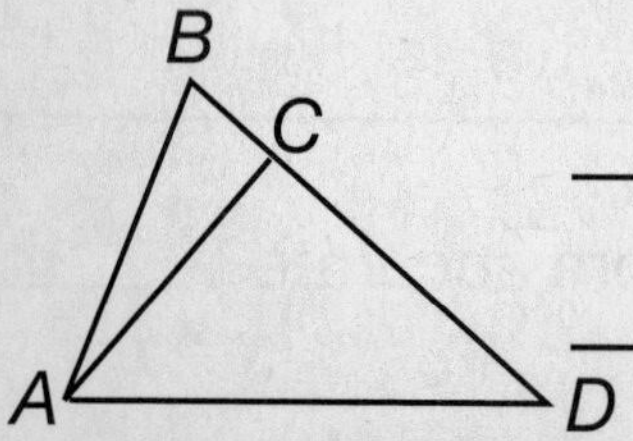

____

____

15. Name all of the rays with endpoint *Y*.

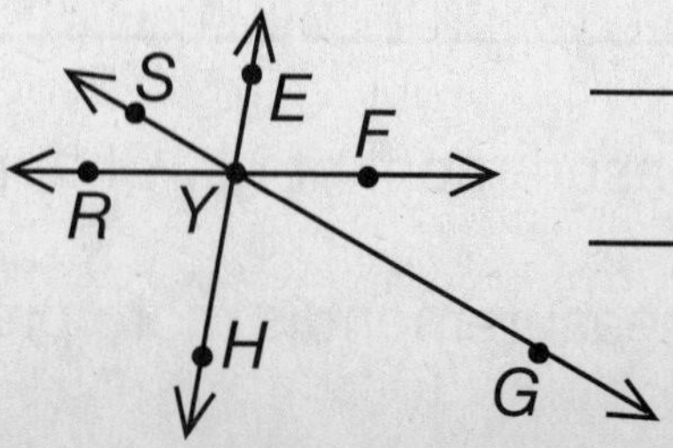

____

____

NAME

SHARPEN YOUR SKILLS

Draw a Diagram

Draw a diagram for each problem.

1. Show the locus of points in a plane 1.5 cm from *P*.

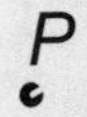

2. Show the locus of points in a plane 0.5 cm from $\overline{AB}$.

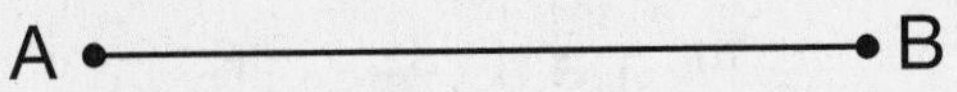

3. Show the locus of points in a plane less than 1.5 cm from $\overline{GR}$.

Draw a diagram and describe the locus.

4. Show six cheerleaders who are 3 feet from the head cheerleader.

H = head cheerleader

1 cm = 3 ft

5. Show the points in a plane 1.5 cm from points *J* and *K*.

6. Show the points in a plane more than 0.5 cm from point *W*.

NAME

SHARPEN YOUR SKILLS

Pairs of Angles

Find the measure of each angle if $m\angle ECD = 65°$ and $\angle ABC$ is a right angle. **Remember** to read $m\angle MKW$ as "the measure of $\angle MKW$."

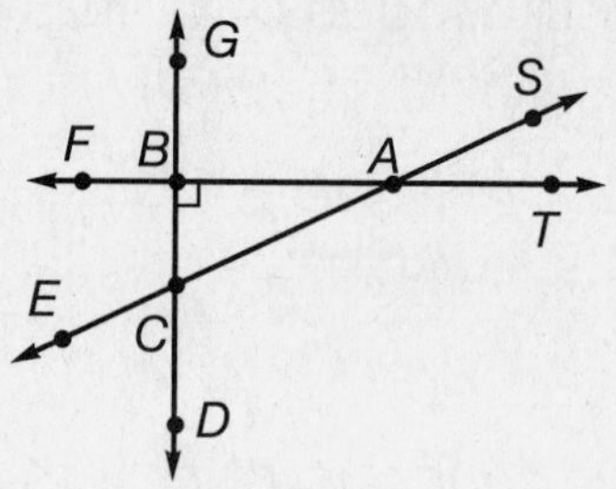

1. $m\angle BCA$ ________
2. $m\angle BAC$ ________
3. $m\angle DCA$ ________
4. $m\angle FBG$ ________
5. $m\angle SAT$ ________

6. Name two pairs of congruent angles.

____

____

____

7. Name three pairs of supplementary angles.

____

____

____

8. Which pairs of angles are complementary?

____

____

____

9. Name three pairs of vertical angles.

____

____

____

Critical Thinking Find each answer.

10. What supplementary angles have equal degree measure?

____

11. What is the degree measure of an angle that is three times its supplement?

____

NAME

SHARPEN YOUR SKILLS

Parallel Lines and Angles

In the figure at the right, lines p and q are parallel, $m\angle BCA = 60°$, and $\angle BAC$ is a right angle. Find the measure of each angle without measuring.

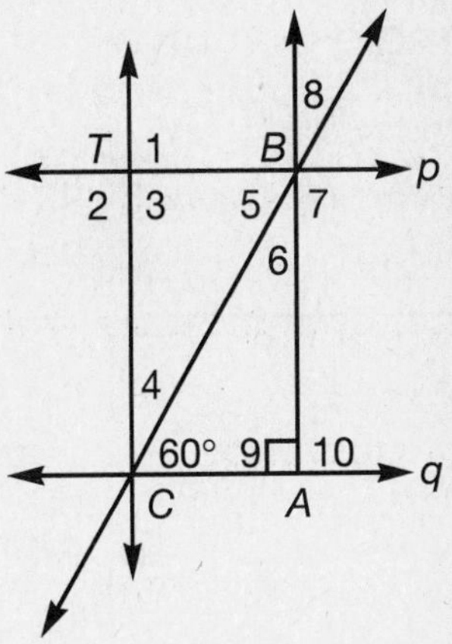

1. $m\angle 6$ ________

2. $m\angle 5$ ________

3. $m\angle 9$ ________

4. $m\angle 8$ ________

In the figure at the right, $\overline{EF} \parallel \overline{HG}$ and $\overline{EH} \parallel \overline{FG}$; $m\angle EFX = 40°$; $m\angle FXE = 80°$. Find each measure.

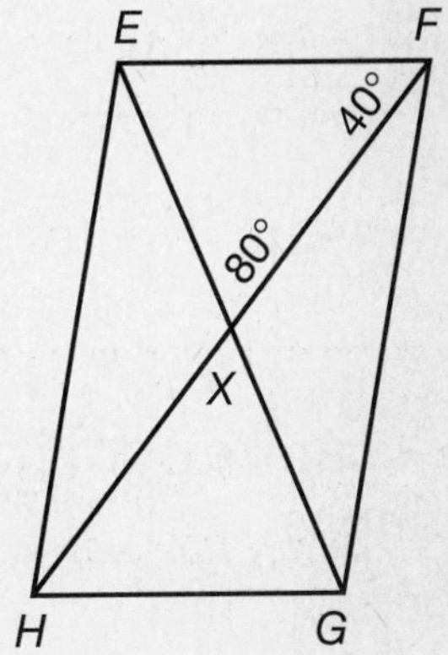

5. $m\angle FEX$ ________

6. $m\angle XGH$ ________

7. $m\angle XHG$ ________ **8.** $m\angle HXG$ ________

9. $m\angle EXH$ ________ **10.** $m\angle FXG$ ________

Mixed Practice Use the given figure to complete each statement.

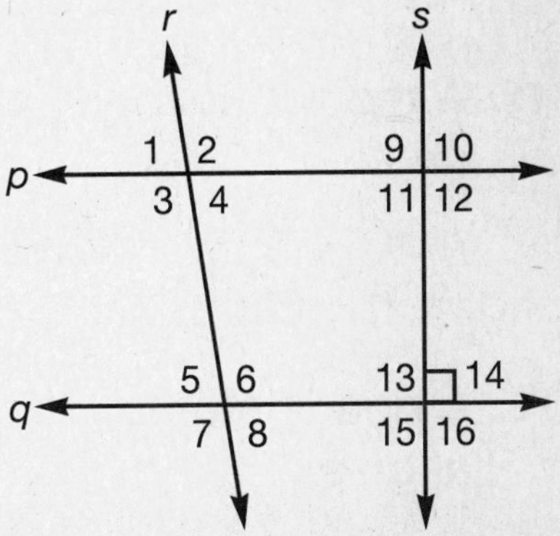

11. $\angle 2$ and $\angle 6$ are ________________

12. $\angle 16$ is a ________ angle.

13. $\angle 5$ and $\angle 8$ are ________________

14. $\angle 3$ and $\angle 4$ are ________________

15. $\angle 3$ and $\angle 6$ are ________________

NAME

Angles in Polygons

SHARPEN YOUR SKILLS

Tell whether you would use mental math, paper or pencil, or a calculator. Determine the number of sides of the regular polygon with a central angle of a given measure.

1. 45°
2. 36°
3. 72°
4. 40°
5. 20°
6. 60°
7. 24°
8. 90°

Tell whether the following figures are possible. Explain.

9. A parallelogram with no right angles
10. A pentagon with five obtuse angles
11. A regular hexagon with an acute angle
12. A regular decagon with a central angle of 45°
13. A quadrilateral with four 90° angles
14. A regular octagon with two acute angles

NAME

SHARPEN YOUR SKILLS

Circles

For Exercises 1–6 use the given approximation for π to find the circumference. Tell whether you would use mental math, paper and pencil, or a calculator.

1. $r = 5$ in.
   $\pi \approx 3.14$

   ______

2. $r = 21$ cm
   $\pi \approx \frac{22}{7}$

   ______

3. $r = 1.6$ ft
   $\pi \approx 3.1416$

   ______

4. $d = 35$ yd
   $\pi \approx \frac{22}{7}$

   ______

5. $d = 15$ m
   $\pi \approx 3.14$

   ______

6. $r = 100.4$ mm
   $\pi \approx 3.1416$

   ______

For Exercises 7–15 find the measure of each angle if $m\angle BOA = 100°$; $\overline{BC}$, $\overline{AF}$, $\overline{GO}$ are parallel; $m\angle FOD = m\angle DOG$.

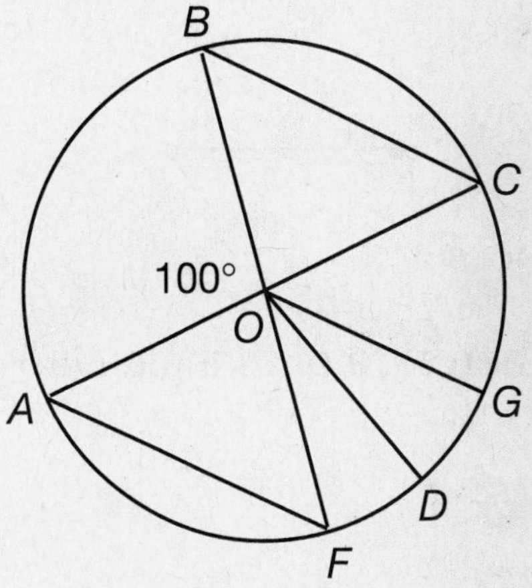

7. $\angle BOG$ ______

8. $\angle BOC$ ______

9. $\angle COG$ ______

10. $\angle FOA$ ______

11. $\angle FOC$ ______

12. $\angle FOG$ ______

13. $\angle BCO$ ______

14. $\angle AOG$ ______

15. $\angle FOG$ ______

Mental Math Without using a calculator, choose the best answer.

16. The area of a circle with a radius of 5.1 cm is given by a calculator with which of the following displays?

816.714 408.357 81.6714 163.3428

NAME

Basic Geometric Constructions

SHARPEN YOUR SKILLS

Construct a segment or an angle congruent to each of the following and bisect it.

1. $\overline{XM}$

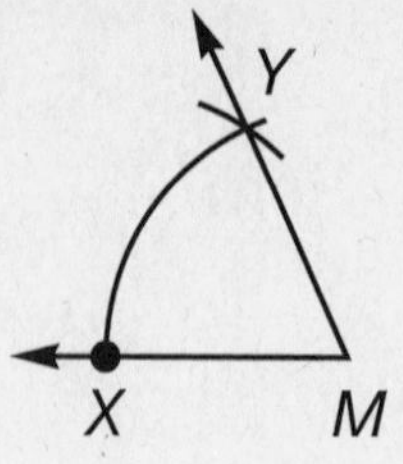

2. $\overline{MY}$

3. $\angle M$

Construct the bisector of each of the following.

4. $\overline{JK}$

5. $\angle KJL$

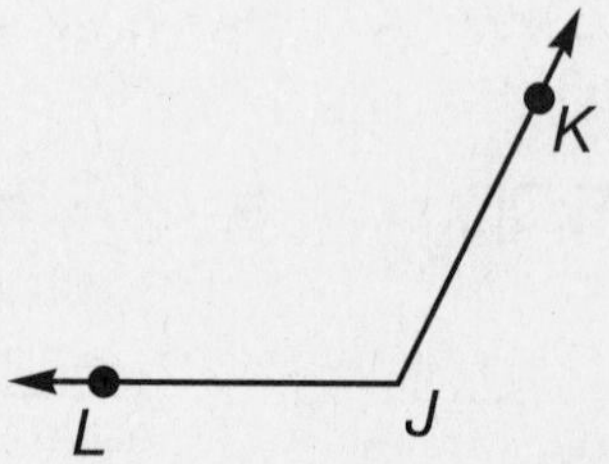

6. Each side of triangle *DEF*

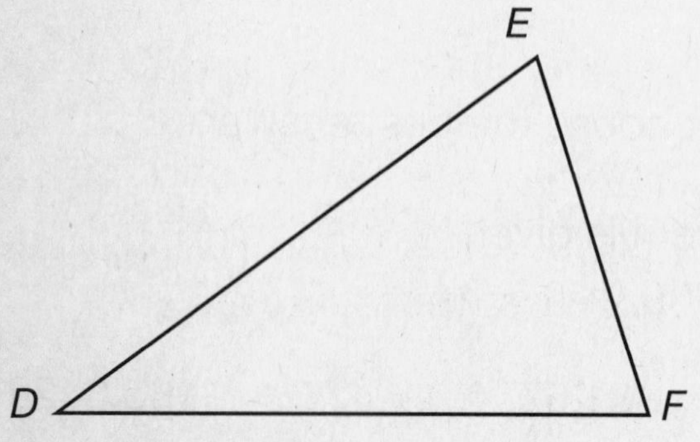

7. Each angle of triangle *RST*

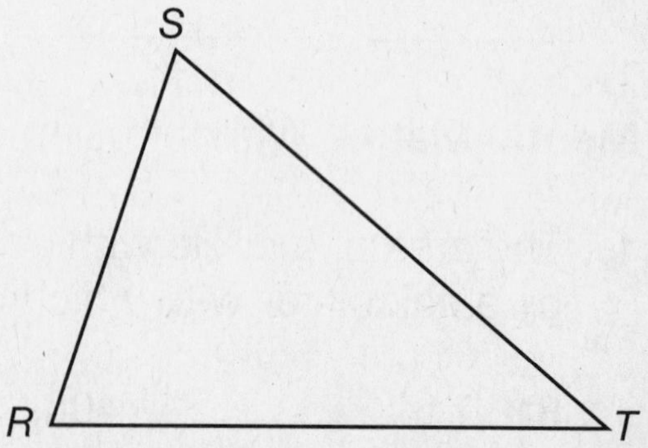

NAME

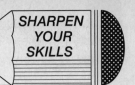

SHARPEN YOUR SKILLS

Constructing Triangles

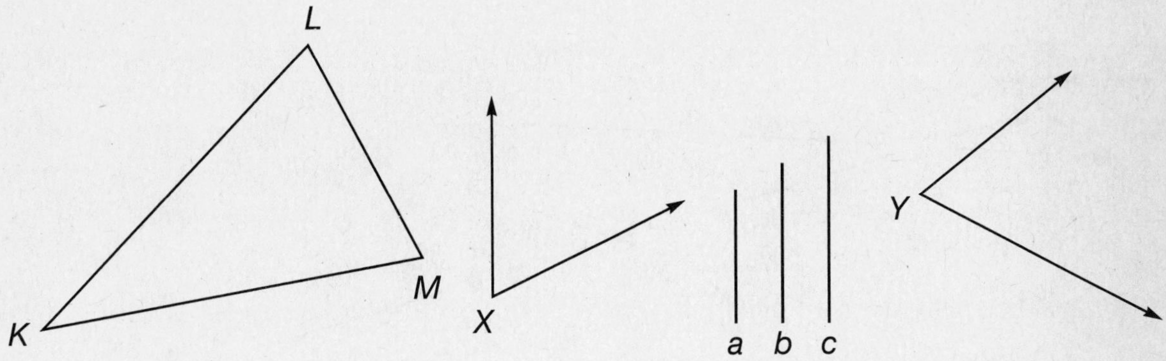

Construct a triangle congruent to $\triangle KLM$ using only the parts given.

1. $\overline{KL}$, $\overline{KM}$, and $\overline{ML}$

2. $\overline{KM}$, $\angle M$, and $\overline{ML}$

Construct a triangle using only the parts given.

3. Sides *a*, *b*, and *c*

4. $\angle X$ between sides *b* and *c*

5. $\angle Y$ between sides *a* and *b*

6. Side *b* between $\angle X$ and $\angle Y$

NAME

Draw a Diagram

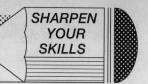

SHARPEN YOUR SKILLS

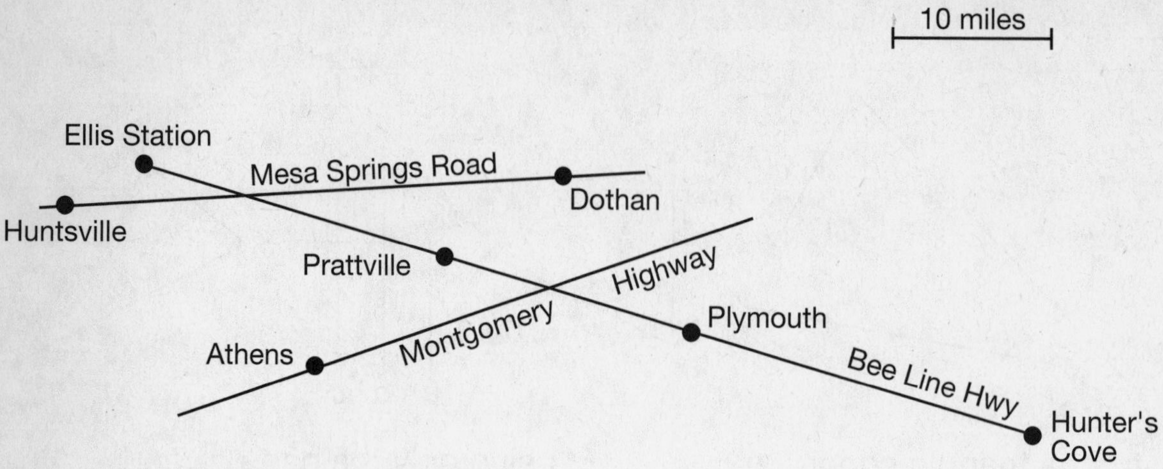

Trace the map above. Then answer these questions.

1. Stacy lives as far from Athens as from Prattville. Construct the locus of points equally distant from Athens and Prattville. Draw the locus on the map.

2. Stacy also lives as far from Huntsville as from Plymouth. Construct the locus of points equally distant from Huntsville and Plymouth. Draw the locus on the map.

3. Mark the location of Stacy's house on the map. About how many miles from Athens is Stacy's home?

____

4. About how many miles from Huntsville is Stacy's home?

____

5. About how far is Huntsville from Dothan?

____

6. A television tower located in Hunter's Cove can transmit 50 miles in all directions. What towns are outside the transmission range of the tower?

____

NAME

SHARPEN YOUR SKILLS

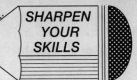

Relating Geometric Solids to Real-World Objects

Name each solid.

1. ____________

2. ____________

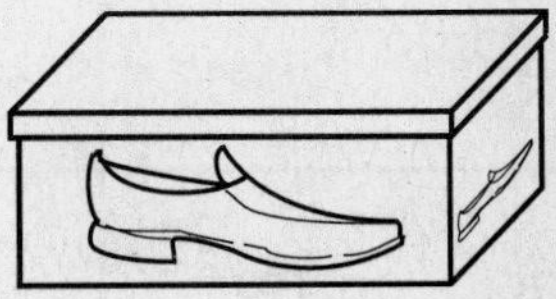

3. ____________

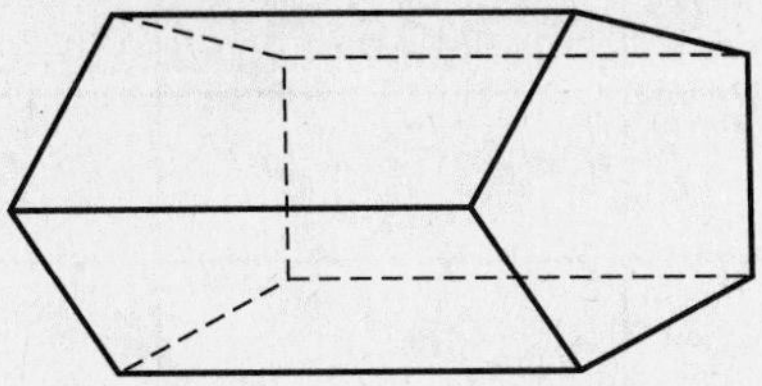

4. ____________

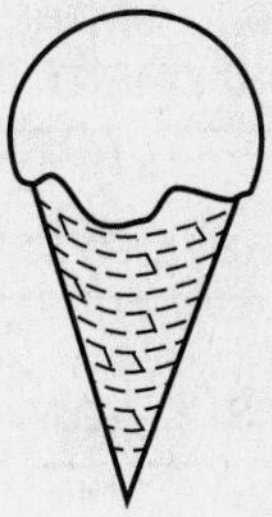

5. ____________

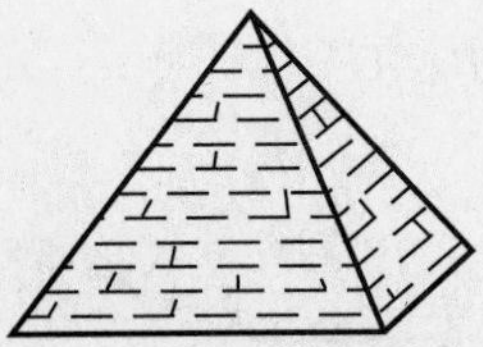

6. ____________

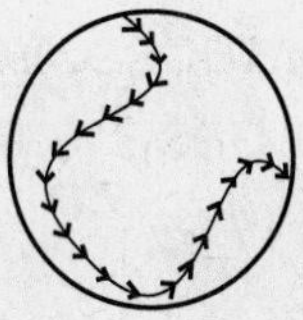

7. If the base of a pyramid is heptagonal, how many faces does the pyramid have?

____

8. If the bases of a prism are octagonal, how many faces does the prism have?

____

9. Sketch a square prism.

10. Sketch a hexagonal pyramid.

NAME

SHARPEN YOUR SKILLS

Make a Table

Complete the table for prisms and pyramids. Let *n* be the number of sides of the polygons that form the base.

Polyhedron	*n*	Number of faces (*f*)	Number of vertices (*v*)	Number of edges (*e*)
1. Triangular prism				
2. Rectangular prism				
3. Octagonal prism			16	
4. Pentagonal pyramid				10
5. Nonagonal pyramid	9		10	
6. Decagonal pyramid	10			20

7. How many faces, vertices, and edges will a pyramid have if the base is a polygon with 50 sides?

____

8. Write an equation that expresses the relationship between the number of sides on the base of a prism and the number of faces. Write a similar equation for pyramids.

____

9. Write an equation that expresses the relationship between the number of sides on the base of a prism and the number of vertices. Write a similar equation for pyramids.

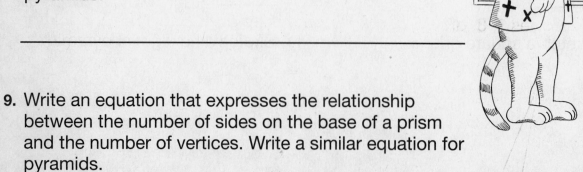

____

Use after pages 324–325.

NAME

SHARPEN YOUR SKILLS

Patterns for Geometric Solids

Match each figure with a solid.

1. 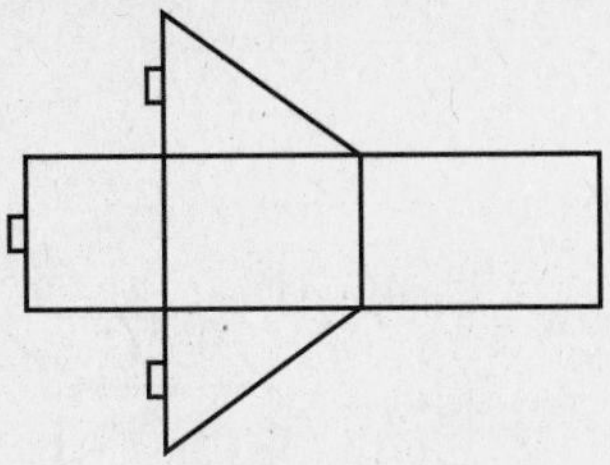 ______

2. 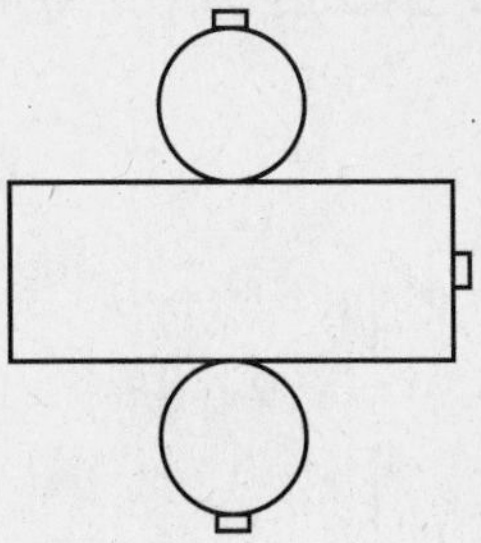 ______

3. 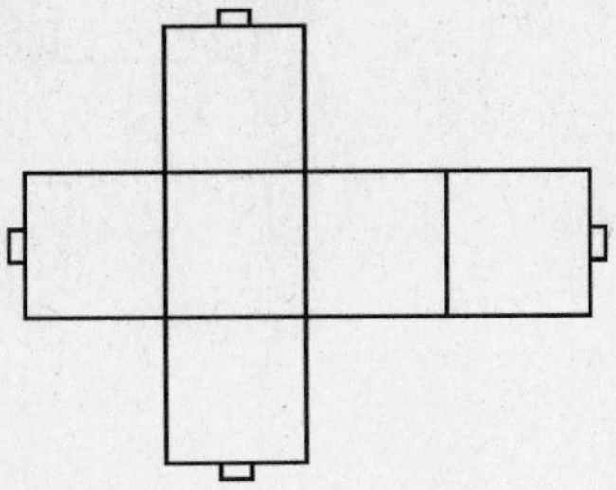 ______

4. 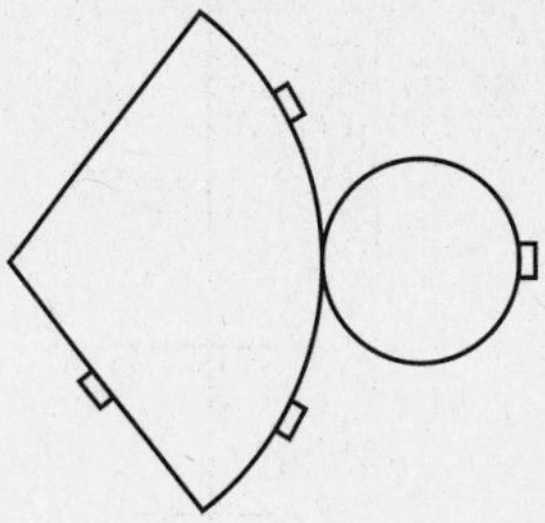 ______

a. 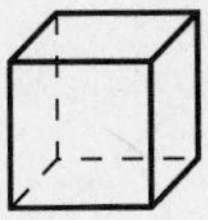

b. 

c. 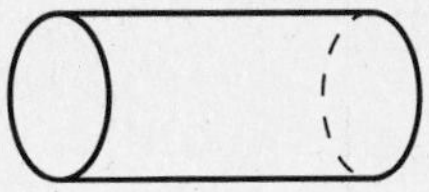

d. 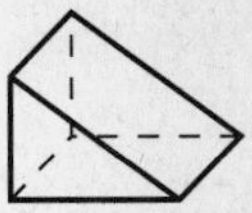

Name the solid that each pattern represents.

5. 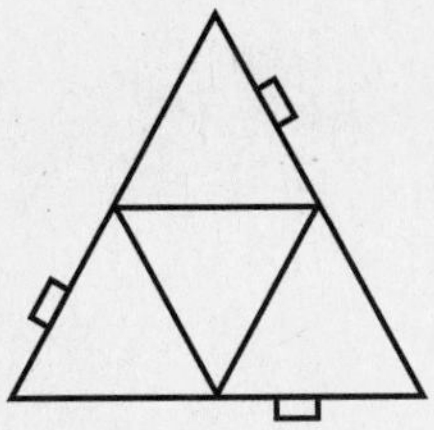

____

____

6. 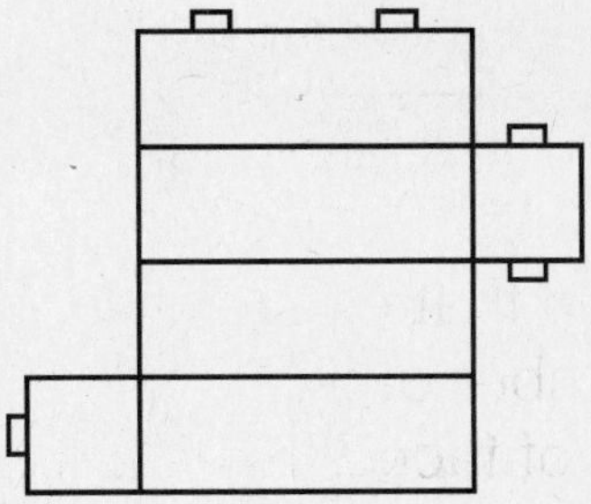

____

____

For Exercises 7–8, draw a pattern for each solid.

7. 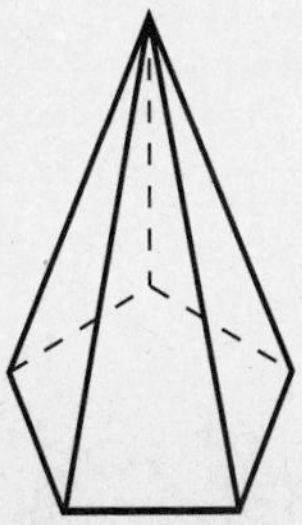

8. 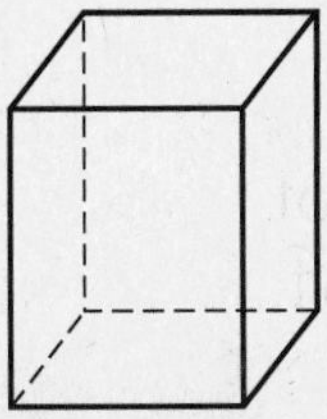

Use after pages 326–329.

NAME

SHARPEN YOUR SKILLS

Drawing Three-Dimensional Figures

Draw the top, bottom, and all side views to give an accurate impression of the figure.

1.

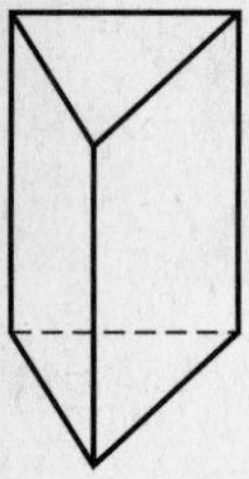

2.

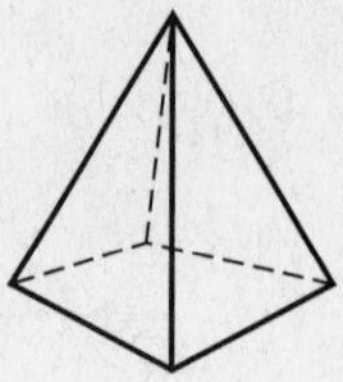

3.

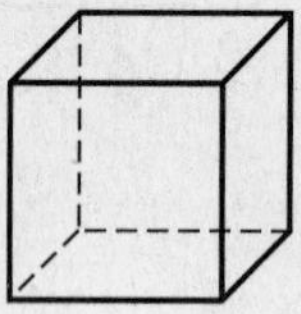

4.

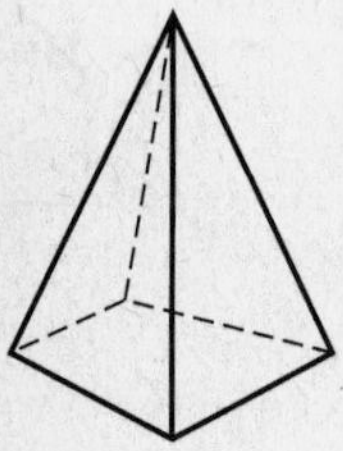

5.

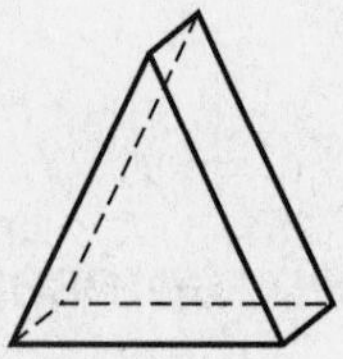

6.

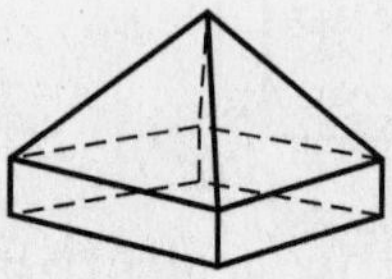

7.

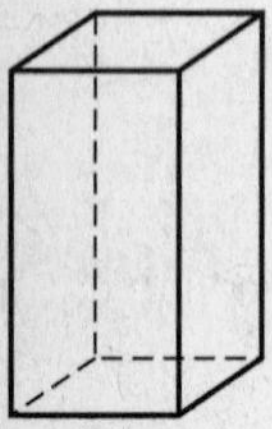

8.

NAME

SHARPEN YOUR SKILLS

Measurement and Circles

Complete the following table, where *r, d, C,* and *A* represent the radius, diameter, circumference, and area of the circle. Round answers to hundredths where appropriate.
Remember to choose $\frac{22}{7}$ or 3.14 for π.

r	*d*	*C*	*A*
1.	10.4	**2.**	**3.**
4.	**5.**	28.89	**6.**
2.1	**7.**	**8.**	**9.**
10.	**11.**	**12.**	154

Find the area of the circle having the given dimension.

13. d = 10 in. ____________

14. r = 11 ____________

15. d = 6.8 m ____________

16. r = 17 mi ____________

Solve each problem. Use $\frac{22}{7}$ for π.

17. A circular patio has a radius of 12 ft. What is the area of the patio?

____

18. The bottom of a large planter is circular with a diameter of 26 in. What is the area of the bottom?

____

NAME

SHARPEN YOUR SKILLS

Measurement of Parallelograms and Triangles

Find the area of each polygon. Tell whether you used mental math or paper and pencil.

1.
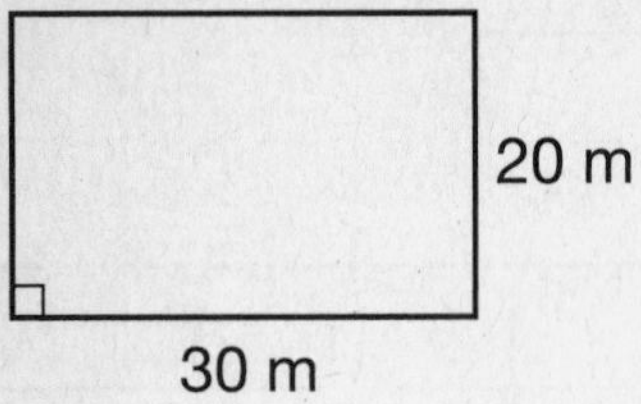

2.
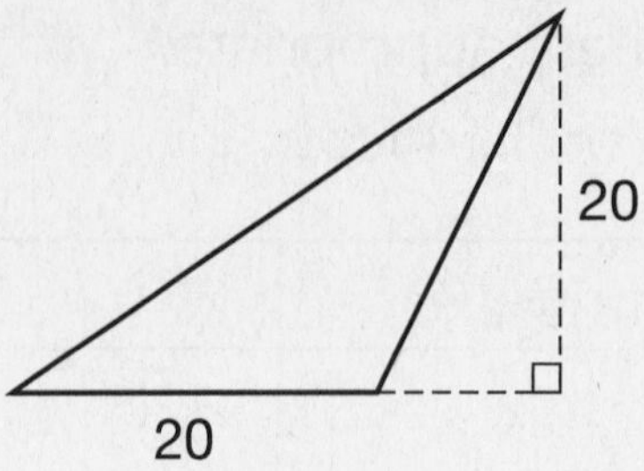

3.
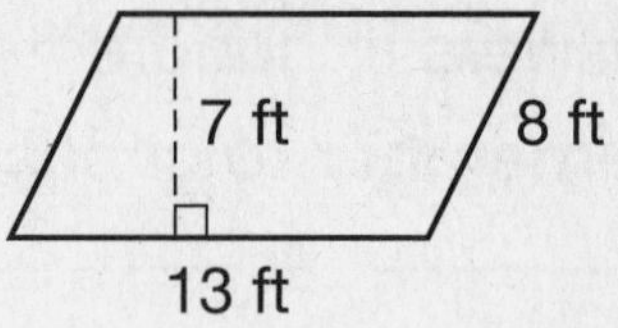

4. A triangle with base 45 in. and height 24 in.

5. A parallelogram with base 1.5 and height 2

6. A triangle with base 3.2 cm and 3.4 cm

Each side of a rectangle is doubled. Answer each question.

7. By what factor is the perimeter multiplied?

8. By what factor is the area multiplied?

Find each answer. **Remember** to draw a figure from the given information.

9. Find the area of a square garden, 25 m on a side.

10. Find the perimeter of a square table, 120 in. by 120 in.

11. The area of a square garden is 49 sq yd. What is the length of a side?

12. Find the length of a rectangle with width 12 units and area 120 square units.

NAME

SHARPEN YOUR SKILLS

Measurement of Trapezoids and Irregular Figures

Find the perimeter and the area to the nearest tenth.
Tell whether you use mental math or paper and pencil.

1.

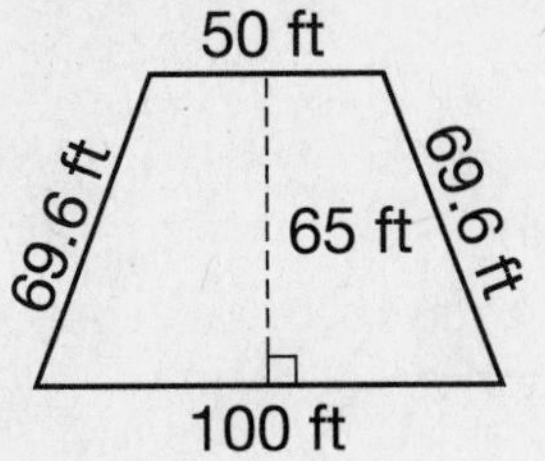

P = ________________

A = ________________

2.

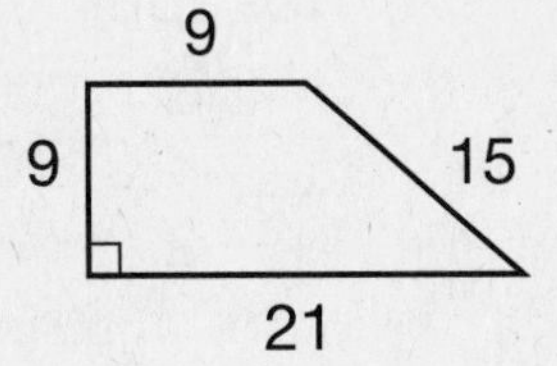

P = ________________

A = ________________

3.

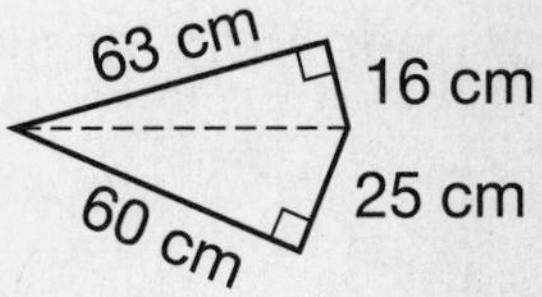

P = ________________

A = ________________

4.

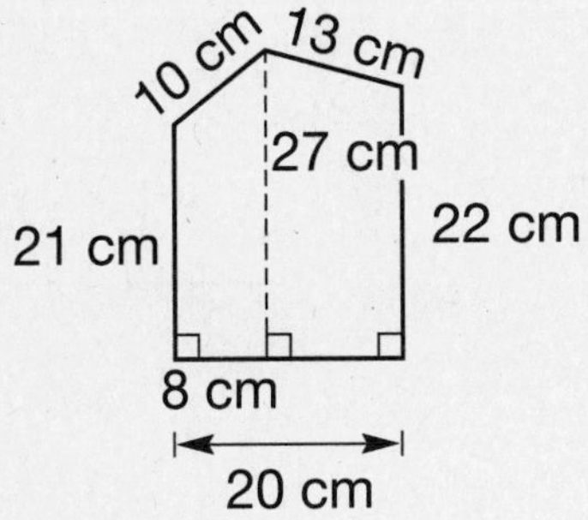

P = ________________

A = ________________

5.

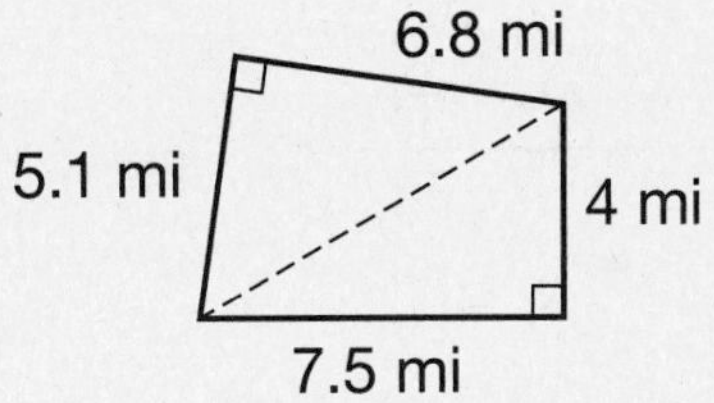

P = ________________

A = ________________

6.

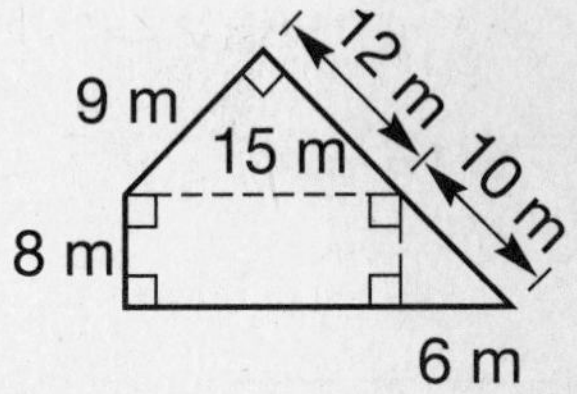

P = ________________

A = ________________

Find the area.

7. A trapezoid with bases 40 and 50 and a height of 70

____

8. A trapezoid with bases 1.5 m and 2.5 m and a height of 2 m

____

9. A trapezoid with bases 20 in. and 30 in. and a height of 30 in.

____

Mixed Practice Find each answer.

10. A rectangle is divided into four smaller rectangles. The areas of three of the rectangles are shown. Find the area of the fourth rectangle.

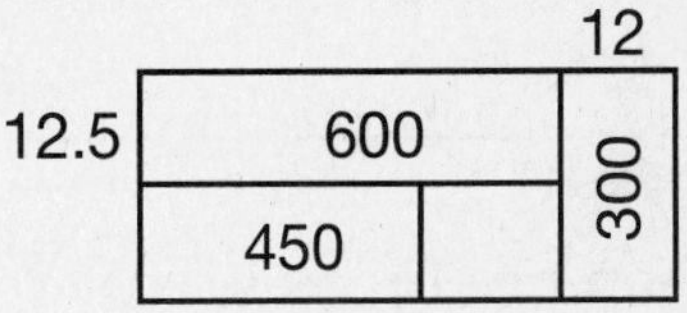

____

11. Find a point X on $\overline{BC}$ so that $\overline{AX}$ divides the polygon into two regions of equal area.

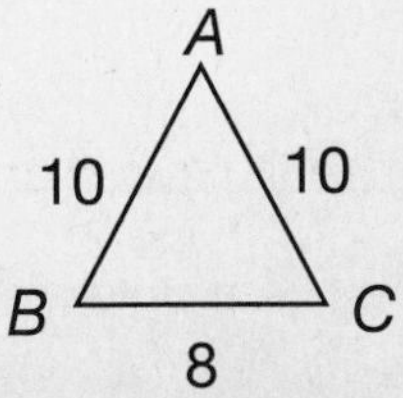

NAME

SHARPEN YOUR SKILLS

Use Data from a Diagram

Describe the shape used to estimate the area. Trace the shapes on centimeter graph paper. Let each square equal one square unit. Estimate the area. **Remember** to label the units in your answer.

1.

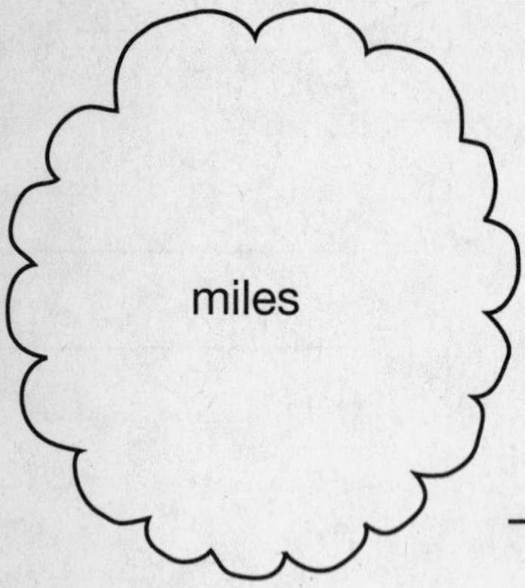

____

____

2.

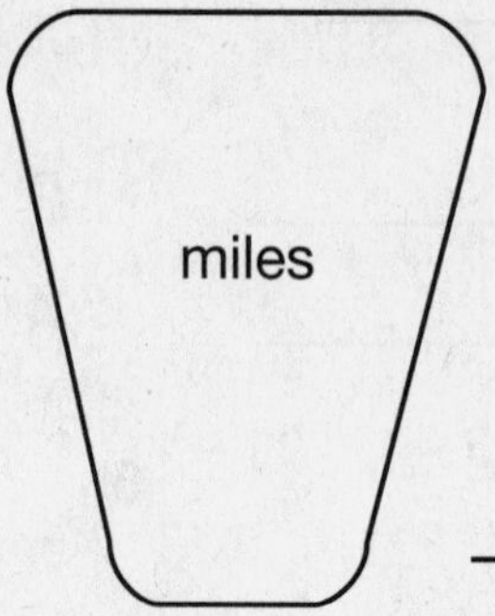

____

____

3.

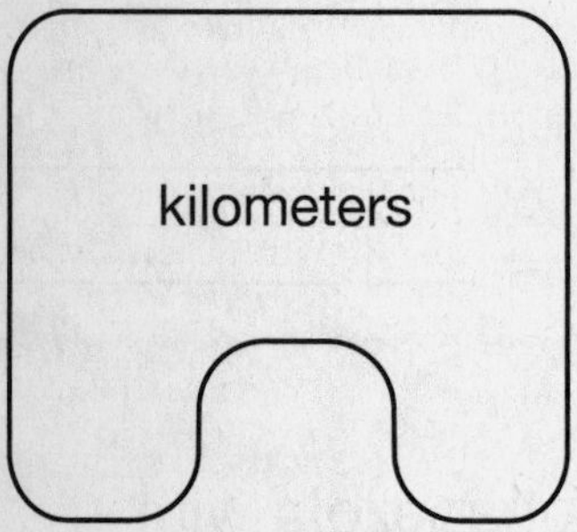

____

____

4.

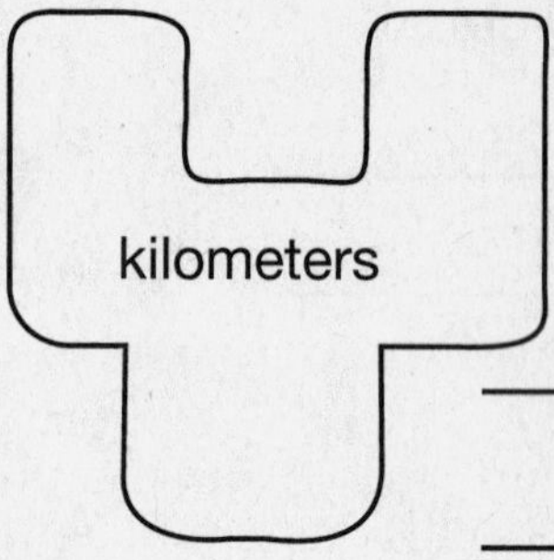

____

____

5. What are the dimensions of a box just large enough to hold a thousand pennies in a single stack?

____

6. How many pennies would there be in a stack as high as a man 6 ft tall?

____

7. How many pennies would there be in a stack as high as a 30 ft building?

____

8. What are the dimensions of a box just large enough to hold 10,000 pennies?

____

____

NAME

Volume of Prisms and Cylinders

SHARPEN YOUR SKILLS

Find the volume of each prism or cylinder to the nearest hundredth. (Let $\pi = 3.14$.)
Remember to label the units in your answer.

1.
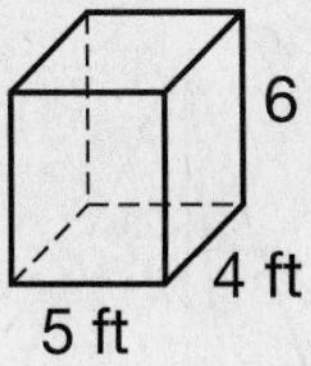

2.
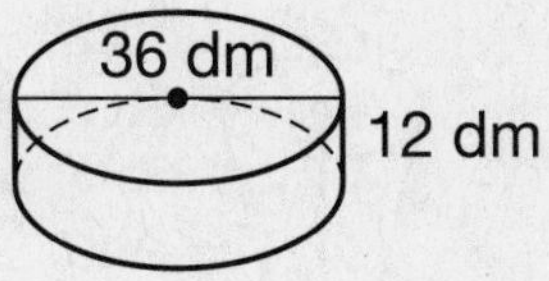

3.
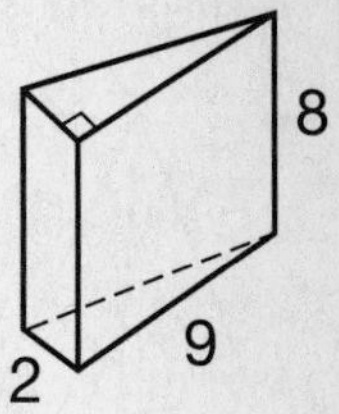

4.
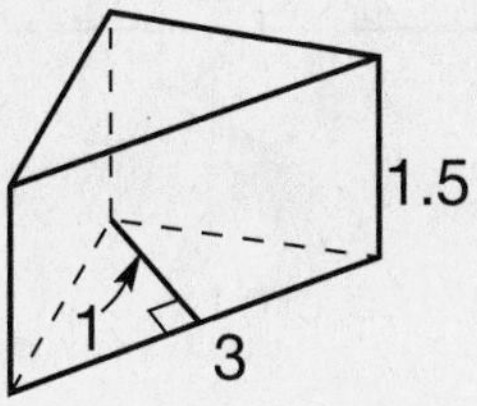

5.
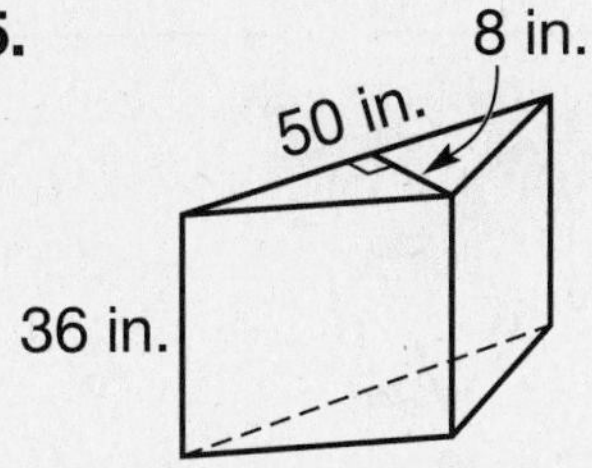

6.
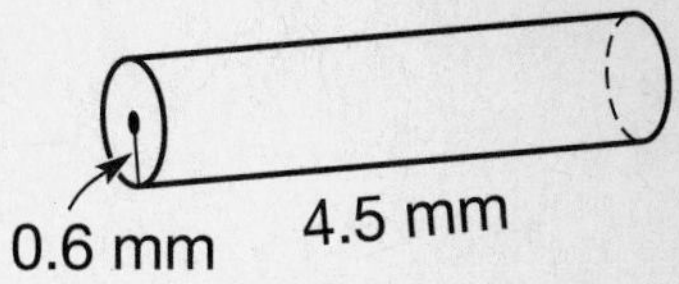

7. A cylinder with diameter 15 inches and height 3 inches

8. A cube with edge 4 feet

9. A rectangular prism with base area 14 mm^2 and height 7 mm

10. A cylinder with diameter 6 mm and height 21 mm

NAME

SHARPEN YOUR SKILLS

Volume of Pyramids and Cones

Find the volume of each figure to the nearest hundredth. (Let $\pi = 3.14$). Tell whether you used paper and pencil or calculator.

1.

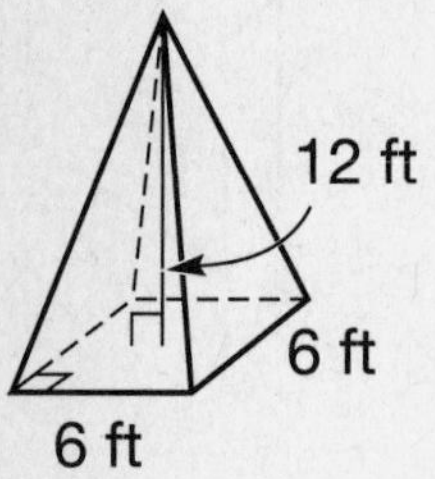

2.

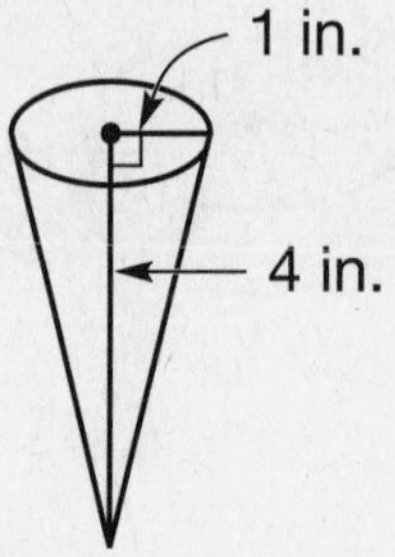

3.

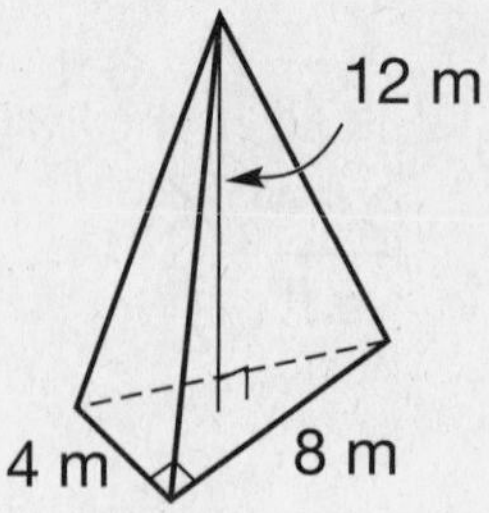

4.

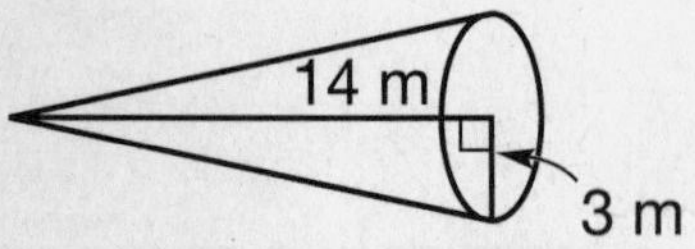

5.

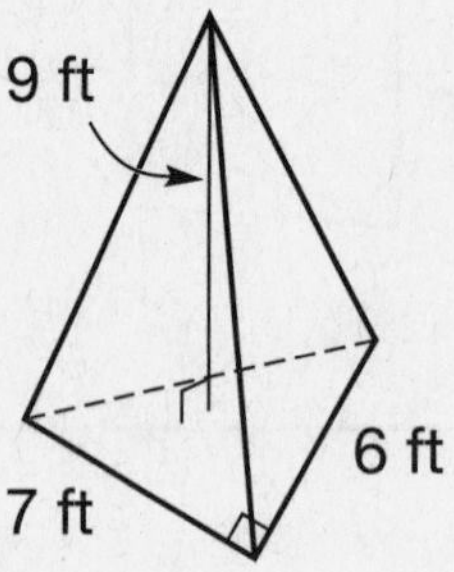

6.

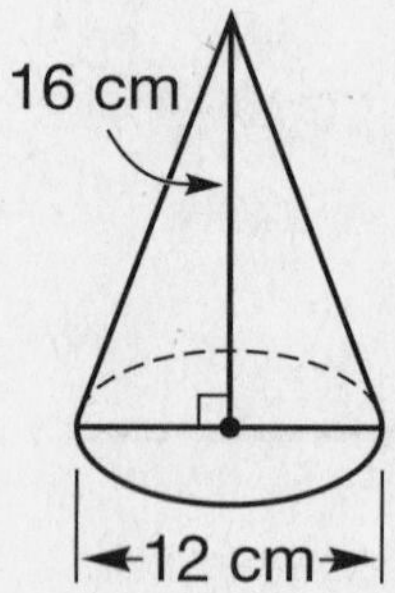

7. A pentagonal pyramid with base area 30 sq ft and height 15 ft

8. A triangular pyramid with base area 900 sq ft and height 12 ft

9. A cone with diameter 6 inches and height 15 inches

10. A cone with radius 7.5 cm and height 18 cm

NAME

SHARPEN YOUR SKILLS

Use a Formula

Use a formula to solve each problem. **Remember** to label the units of the answer. Write the formula for each problem. Use 3.14 for π.

1. A silo in the shape of a cylinder is 40 meters high and has a radius of 30 meters. Find the volume of the silo.

____

2. A kickball in the shape of a sphere has a radius of 10 cm. Find the volume of the kickball to the nearest whole number.

____

3. A cylinder has a height of 4 cm and a radius of 3 cm. Find the volume of the cylinder to the nearest whole number.

____

4. A sphere has a radius of 9 cm. Find the volume of the sphere to the nearest whole number.

____

5. A hat box in the shape of a cylinder has a radius of 20 cm and is 20 cm high. Find the volume of the hat box to the nearest whole number.

____

6. A sphere has a radius of 12 cm. Find the volume of the sphere to the nearest cubic centimeter.

____

7. A cylinder has a diameter of 10 cm and a height of 6 cm. Find the volume of the cylinder to the nearest cubic centimeter.

____

8. A sphere has a diameter of 40 m. Find the volume of the sphere to the nearest cubic meter.

____

Use after pages 366–367.

NAME

SHARPEN YOUR SKILLS

Surface Area of Prisms

Find the surface area of each prism.
Remember to label units in your answers.

1.

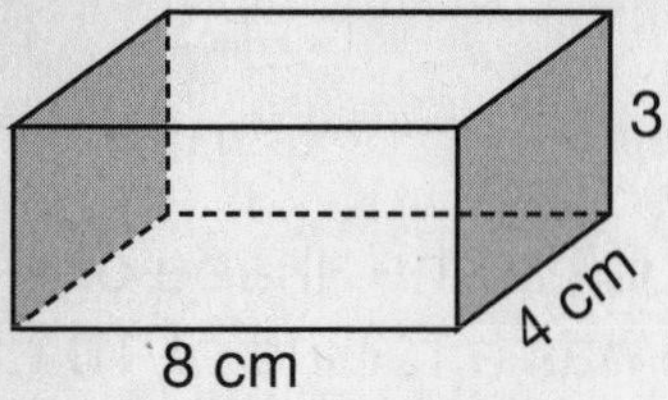

____

2.

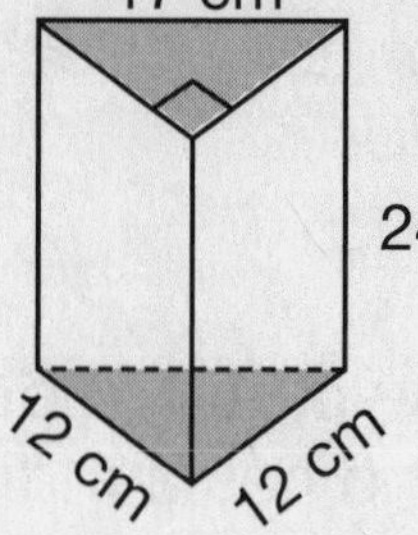

____

3.

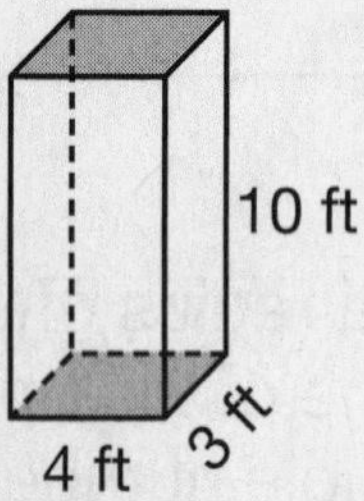

____

4.

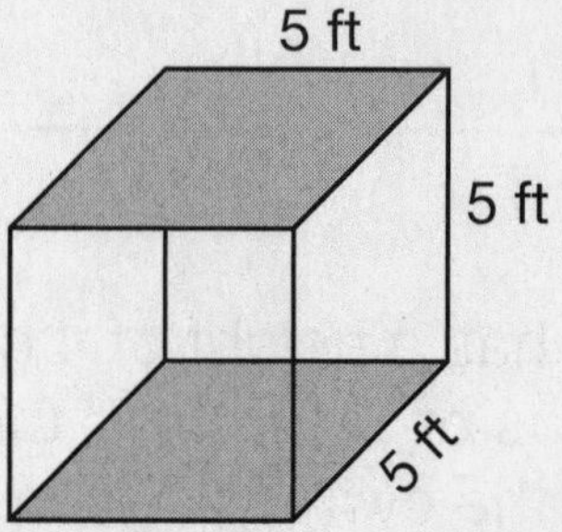

____

5.

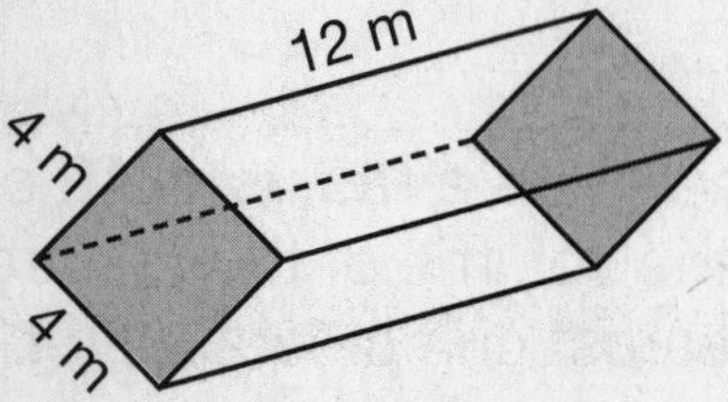

____

6.

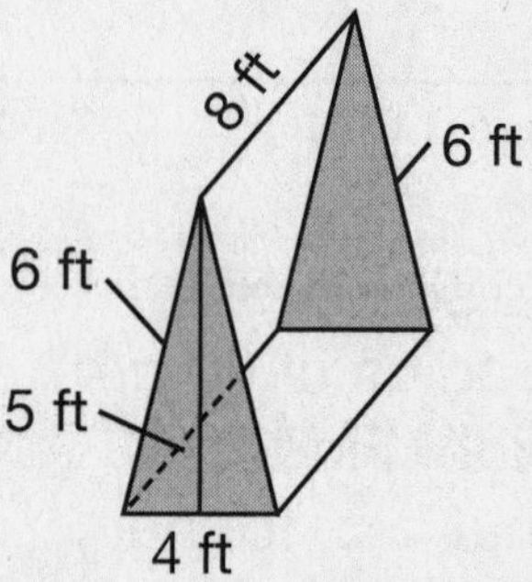

____

Mixed Practice Find the surface area and volume of each figure.

7.

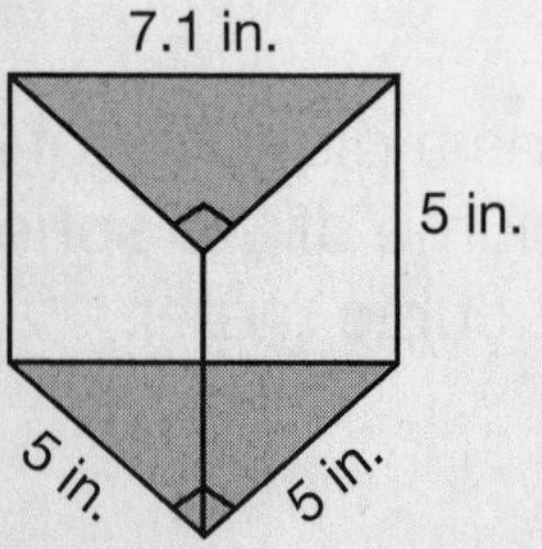

____

____

8.

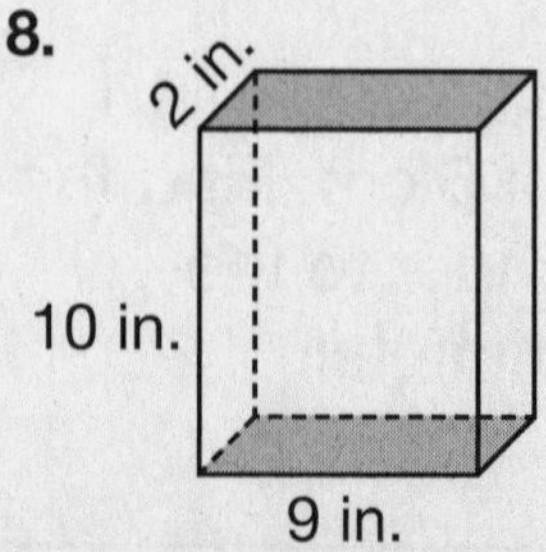

____

____

NAME

SHARPEN YOUR SKILLS

Surface Area of Pyramids

Find the surface area of each pyramid. **Remember** to label your answers.

1.

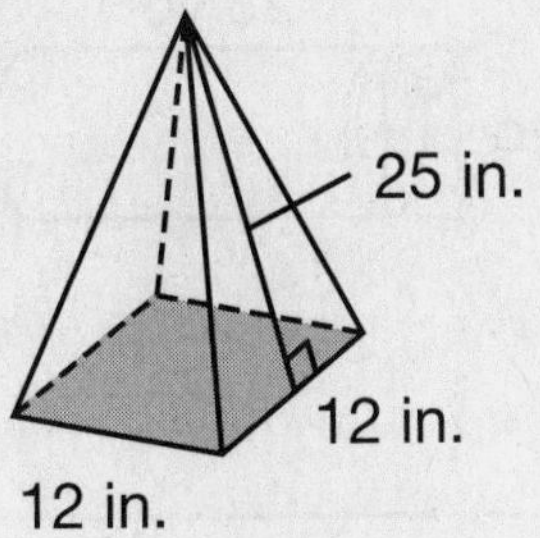

____

2.

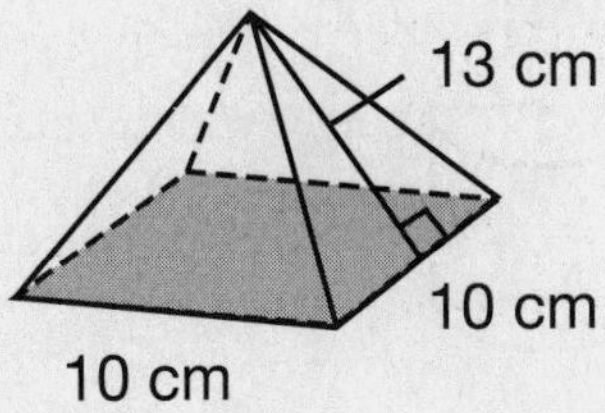

____

3.

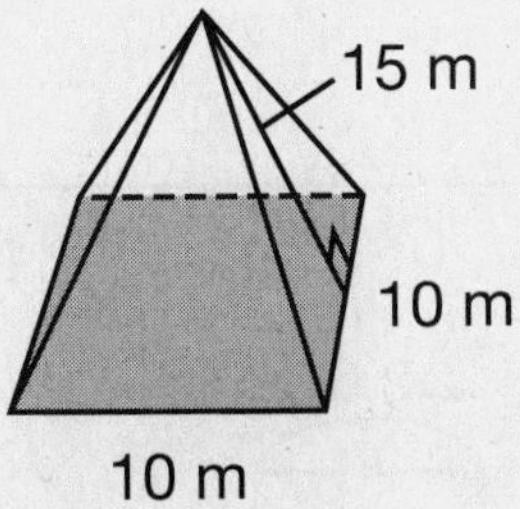

____

4.

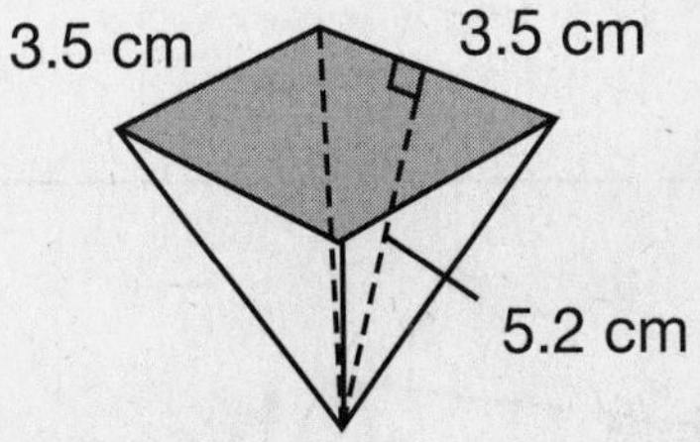

____

5.

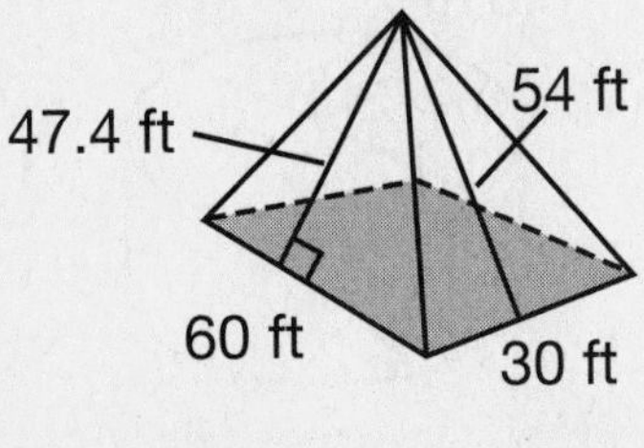

____

6.

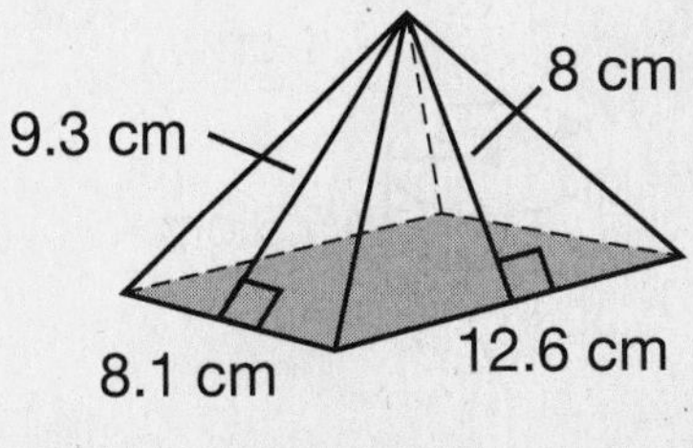

____

NAME

Surface Area of Cylinders

SHARPEN YOUR SKILLS

Find the surface area. Use 3.14 for π. Round to the nearest hundredth. Tell whether you use paper and pencil or calculator. **Remember** to label units in your answer.

1.

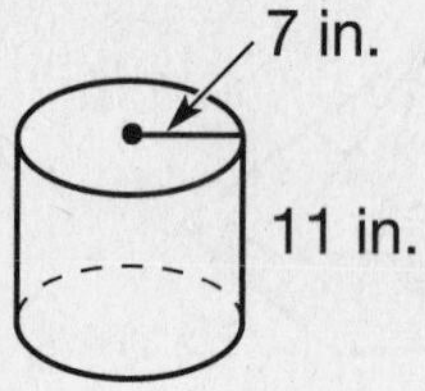

____

2.

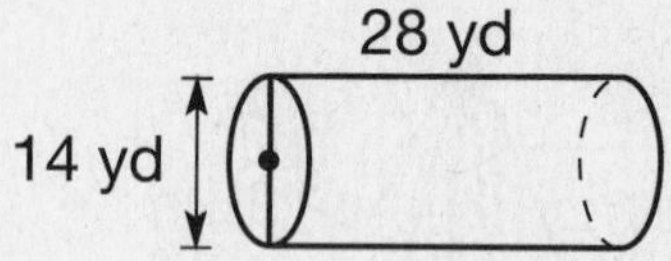

____

3.

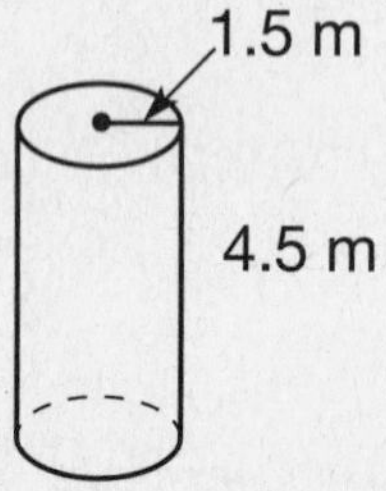

____

4.

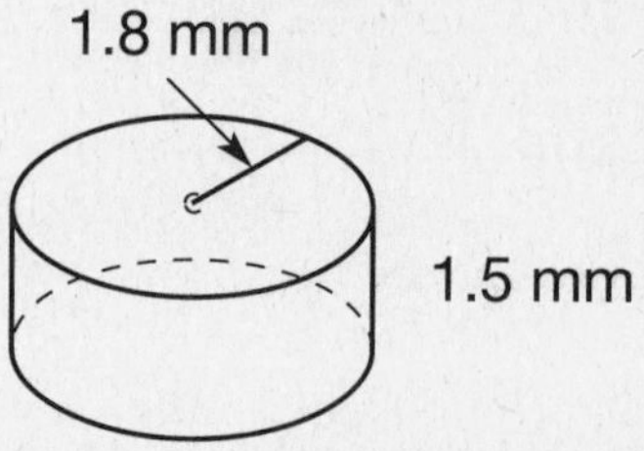

____

5.

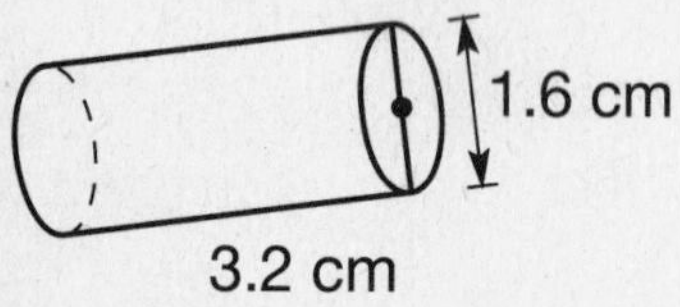

____

6.

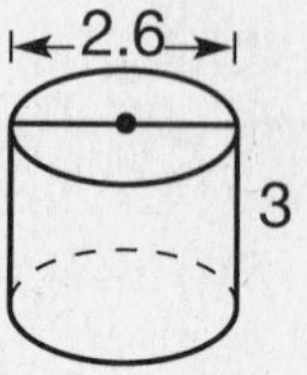

____

Mixed Practice Find the surface area and the volume of each cylinder.

7.

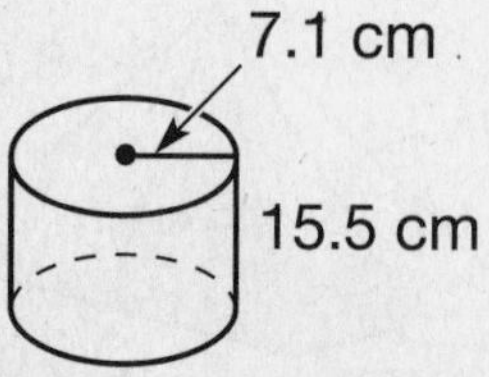

SA = ______________________

V = ______________________

8.

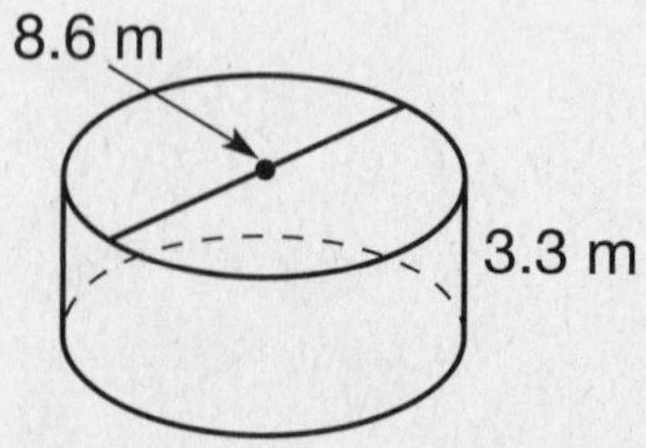

SA = ______________________

V = ______________________

NAME ______________________

SHARPEN YOUR SKILLS

Try and Check

Use the try and check method to solve each problem. A table may be helpful.

1. A landscaper has 500 yards of fencing. He wants to enclose a rectangular area. What dimensions of a garden plot will yield the greatest area without requiring additional fencing?

____

2. Find two numbers whose sum is 7 and whose product is as large as possible.

____

3. Find the largest possible shaded area for a circle inscribed in a square that measures 4 inches on a side. Use 3.14 for π.

____

4. A rectangular plot of land beside a river is to be fenced on 3 sides for a pasture. The side along the river bank requires no fencing. If 450 meters of fencing are available for the other 3 sides, what is the largest possible area for the pasture?

____

5. You want to mail a set of 64 one-inch cube-shaped blocks in the smallest possible box. What are the dimensions of the box you need that would have the least surface area?

____

NAME

SHARPEN YOUR SKILLS

Rational Number System

Solve for *n*. Tell what property is illustrated.

1. $n + 5.9 = 5.9 + 3.4$

2. $12 \times (n \times 3) = (12 \times 6) \times 3$

3. $8.46 \times n = 5 \times 8.46$

4. $8.4 \times n = 0$

5. $\frac{16}{2} \times \text{n} = \frac{16}{2}$

6. $(2.4 + n) + 5.9 = 2.4 + (6 + 5.9)$

7. $173.5 + n = 173.5$

8. $2.3 \times 5 + 2.3 \times 3 = n\,(5 + 3)$

9. $\frac{3}{4} \times \frac{2}{3} = n \times \frac{3}{4}$

10. $(1.5 \times 4) \times n = 1.5 \times (4 \times 3.2)$

Mental Math Use mental math to compute. Tell what property you used.

11. $39 + 11 + 53$

12. $7 \times 1.2 + 7 \times 0.8$

13. $6 \times 3\frac{1}{4} \times \frac{1}{6}$

14. 237.482×1

NAME

SHARPEN YOUR SKILLS

Exponents and Powers of Ten

Write in standard form.

1. 10^{-3} ____________________
2. 10^{1} ____________________
3. 10^{8} ____________________
4. 10^{-6} ____________________
5. 10^{-7} ____________________
6. 10^{7} ____________________
7. 10^{5} ____________________
8. 10^{6} ____________________
9. 10^{0} ____________________
10. 10^{-4} ____________________
11. 10^{3} ____________________
12. 10^{-9} ____________________

Write in exponential form.

13. 100 ________
14. 10,000 ________
15. 1,000 ________
16. 10 ________
17. 1 ________
18. 100,000 ________
19. 0.01 ________
20. 0.00001 ________
21. 0.001 ________
22. $\frac{1}{10}$ ________
23. $\frac{1}{10,000}$ ________
24. $\frac{1}{100}$ ________

Solve. Write each answer in exponential form.

25. How many centimeters are there in 1 hectometer?

____

26. How many liters in 1 kiloliter?

____

27. Find the number of millimeters in 100 centimeters.

____

28. Find the number of grams in a hectogram.

____

Use after pages 394–395.

NAME

SHARPEN YOUR SKILLS

Multiplying and Dividing Powers of Ten

Tell whether you would use mental math or paper and pencil. Then write the answer in exponential form.

1. $10^7 \times 10^7$ ________

2. $10^6 \times 10^2$ ________

3. $\frac{10^6}{10^3}$ ________

4. $\frac{1{,}000}{10{,}000}$ ________

5. $10^{-9} \times 10^7$ ________

6. $10^{-5} \times 10^5$ ________

7. $10^0 \times 10^{-3}$ ________

8. $\frac{10{,}000}{100}$ ________

9. $(10^7 \times 10^8) \times 10^{-5}$ ________

10. $10^6 \times (10^8 \times 10^{-3})$ ________

11. 0.1×0.001 ________

12. $10{,}000 \times 0.01$ ________

Divide. Write the answer in exponential form.

13. $\frac{10^6}{10^9}$ ________

14. $\frac{10^2}{10^{-4}}$ ________

15. $0.00001 \div 0.001$ ________

16. $0.001 \div 10{,}000$ ________

17. $\frac{10^{-3}}{10{,}000}$ ________

18. $\frac{10}{0.01}$ ________

Use after pages 396–397.

NAME

SHARPEN YOUR SKILLS

Scientific Notation for Large Numbers

Write each number in standard form.

1. 6.342×10^4 = ____________ **2.** 1.01×10^3 = ____________

3. 13.359×10^6 = ____________ **4.** 45.7×10^5 = ____________

Write each number in scientific notation.

5. 17 = ____________ **6.** 2,300 = ____________

7. 142,000 = ____________ **8.** 43.5 = ____________

The table gives data that can occur for the growth of a population of bacteria.

Complete the table. Write each number in scientific notation.

	Number of hours	Number of bacteria cells	Scientific notation
9.	0	1	
10.	3	510	
11.	6	260,000	
12.	9	130,000,000	
13.	12	69,000,000,000	
14.	15	35,000,000,000,000	

NAME

SHARPEN YOUR SKILLS

Scientific Notation for Small Numbers

Write each number in scientific notation.

1. 0.14 ______
2. 0.0002 ______
3. 0.0091 ______
4. 0.00035 ______
5. 325,000,000 ______
6. 0.000089 ______

Write each number in standard form.

7. 0.6×10^{-1} ______
8. 4.8×10^{-4} ______
9. 5.46×10^{-3} ______
10. 639×10^{-5} ______
11. 2×10^{-7} ______
12. 7.98×10^{-2} ______

The diameters of some virus particles are given in the table below.

Complete the table. Write each number in scientific notation.

	Virus	Diameter of a particle (meters)	Scientific notation (meters)
13.	Yellow fever	0.000000022	
14.	Mumps	0.0000001	
15.	Cowpox	0.00000025	
16.	Foot and mouth disease	0.00000001	

Mixed Practice Write each number in standard form.

17. 8.36×10^{5} ______
18. 3.9×10^{-3} ______
19. 8.752×10^{2} ______
20. 6.71×10^{-5} ______

NAME

SHARPEN YOUR SKILLS

Computing in Scientific Notation

Tell whether you would use mental math, paper and pencil, or a calculator. Then calculate and write answers in scientific notation.

1. 0.0083×72

2. $72{,}000 \times 0.00062$

3. $(1.3 \times 10^{-4}) \times (5.5 \times 10^{6})$

4. $63{,}000 \times 1{,}400$

5. $0.16 \times 0.2 \times 843{,}000$

6. $\frac{70{,}000}{280{,}000}$

7. $\frac{0.0046}{0.00092}$

8. $\frac{0.934}{0.00634}$

9. $\frac{6.8 \times 10^{6}}{3.4 \times 10^{2}}$

10. $\frac{8.28 \times 10^{4}}{2.3 \times 10^{-2}}$

Use scientific notation to compute each answer. Write answers in standard form.

11. The population of the U.S. is about 245,000,000. The area is 9,400,000 km^2. What is the population per square kilometer in the U.S.?

12. In Australia, there are 1.94 people per square kilometer. The area is 7,700,000 km^2. How many people live in Australia?

NAME

Use Data From a Diagram

SHARPEN YOUR SKILLS

Use the diagram to solve the problems. The front of the house is the same as the back. The unseen side is the same as the side shown. The triangular sections in the front and back of the house are part of the walls and not part of the roof.

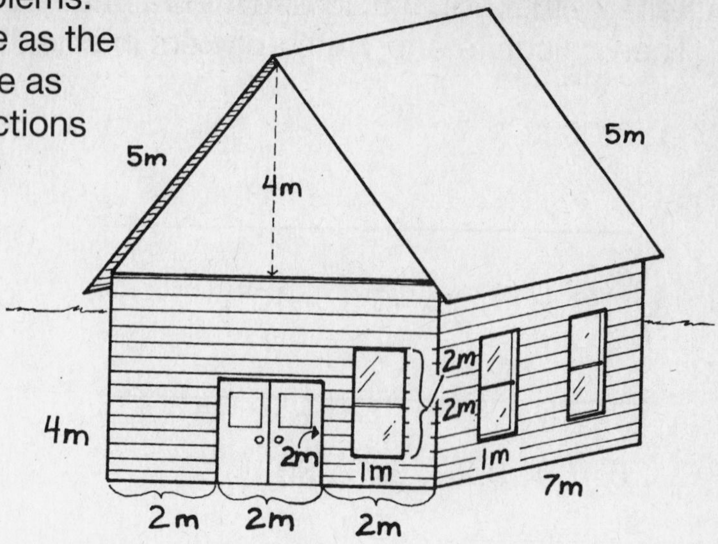

1. What is the surface area of the front of the house including the door and window?

____

2. What is the surface area of the rear of the house including the door and window?

____

3. What is the surface area of each side of the house excluding the windows?

____

4. What is the surface area of the four walls of the house excluding the doors and windows?

____

5. How many square meters of roofing are needed to cover the roof?

____

6. What is the surface area of the doors if there is another set of identical doors at the end of the house?

____

7. How many square meters of solar shield are needed to cover the windows?

____

8. Which is greater, the surface area of the front or of the side of the house including windows and doors, and by how much?

____

NAME ______________________

SHARPEN YOUR SKILLS

Square Roots

Find the square root. Round to the nearest hundredth if necessary.

1. $\sqrt{41}$ ____________
2. $\sqrt{525}$ ____________
3. $\sqrt{289}$ ____________
4. $\sqrt{123}$ ____________
5. $\sqrt{31.2}$ ____________
6. $\sqrt{412}$ ____________
7. $\sqrt{3{,}600}$ ____________
8. $\sqrt{1.21}$ ____________
9. $\sqrt{8{,}888}$ ____________
10. $\sqrt{11}$ ____________
11. $\sqrt{1{,}200}$ ____________
12. $\sqrt{150}$ ____________
13. $\sqrt{4{,}490}$ ____________
14. $\sqrt{3.61}$ ____________
15. $\sqrt{990}$ ____________
16. $\sqrt{7{,}225}$ ____________

Estimation Estimate the square root to the nearest whole number.

17. $\sqrt{31}$ ____________
18. $\sqrt{50}$ ____________
19. $\sqrt{98}$ ____________
20. $\sqrt{77}$ ____________

Solve each problem. **Remember** to use the formula $A = s^2$.

21. A square has area 2.89 cm^2. What is the length of a side?

____

22. Find the area of a square with a side $\sqrt{6.25}$ in. long.

____

Use after pages 408–409.

NAME

Irrational Numbers

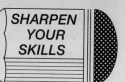

SHARPEN YOUR SKILLS

Write each rational number as a terminating or a repeating decimal.

1. $\frac{9}{10}$ = ______

2. $-\frac{4}{25}$ = ______

3. $3\frac{2}{9}$ = ______

4. $-\frac{5}{11}$ = ______

Tell whether each real number is **rational** or **irrational.**

5. $\sqrt{21}$ ______

6. $\sqrt{5}$ ______

7. -7 ______

8. 22 ______

9. 0 ______

10. $\sqrt{46}$ ______

11. 4.5 ______

12. $7.\overline{3}$ ______

13. $\frac{3}{7}$ ______

14. $4\frac{2}{3}$ ______

15. 8 ______

16. 0.7 ______

17. $1.\overline{6}$ ______

18. -0.333 ______

Write a rational number and an irrational number that are between each pair of numbers.

19. $\sqrt{3}, \sqrt{4}$

______

20. $\sqrt{60}, \sqrt{61}$

______

21. $\sqrt{5}, \sqrt{6}$

______

22. $\sqrt{9}, \sqrt{10}$

______

NAME

Computing with Irrational Numbers

SHARPEN YOUR SKILLS

Compute. Round decimals to the hundredths place.

1. $\sqrt{2} \times \sqrt{4} \times \sqrt{6}$ ________

2. $\sqrt{\frac{16}{49}}$ ________

3. $\sqrt{10} \div \sqrt{5}$ ________

4. $\frac{1}{2}(2\sqrt{5} - 2)$ ________

5. $\sqrt{11} \times \sqrt{11}$ ________

6. $\sqrt{18}$ ________

7. $5\sqrt{3} - 7\sqrt{3}$ ________

8. $\sqrt{\frac{12}{16}}$ ________

9. $\sqrt{16} \times \sqrt{7}$ ________

10. $5\sqrt{2}$ ________

Tell which point on the number line most closely approximates each number.

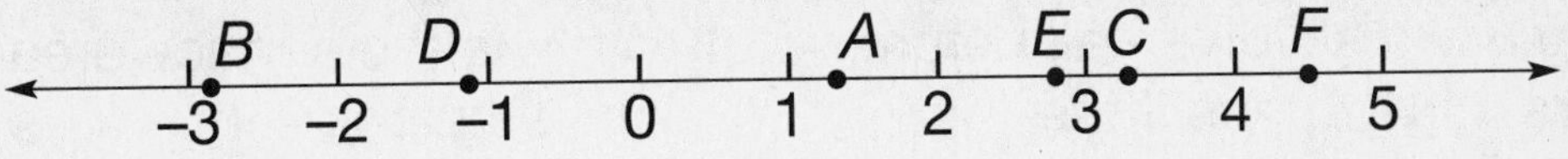

11. $\sqrt{11}$ ____

12. $-\sqrt{5} + 1$ ____

13. $2\sqrt{8} - \sqrt{8}$ ____

14. $\sqrt{2}$ ____

15. $-2\sqrt{2}$ ____

16. $3\sqrt{10} - 5$ ____

Solve each problem.

17. Find the area of a circle with diameter $14\sqrt{2}$ cm.

____

18. Find the perimeter of a triangle with sides having lengths of $3\sqrt{3}$ cm, $4\sqrt{3}$ cm, and $5\sqrt{3}$ cm.

____

NAME

SHARPEN YOUR SKILLS

Use a Formula

Calculator Use a calculator to find answers to the nearest tenth.

Use one of the following formulas to find the answers.

$d = 16t^2$	For the distance of a fall on earth in feet
$d = 0.8t^2$	For the distance of a fall on the moon in meters
$A = \pi r^2$	For the area of a circle
$A = s^2$	For the area of a square
$SA = 6s^2$	For the surface area of a cube

1. How long will it take a baseball to fall from the top of a building 720 ft tall?

____

2. What is the area of the floor of a square room whose walls are 30 feet long?

____

3. How far will a skydiver fall before the parachute opens if the parachute opens 9 seconds after the diver leaves the aircraft?

____

4. What is the surface area of a child's block with edges 5 cm long?

____

5. How far will a camera have fallen if it is dropped from a lunar lander and falls for 20 seconds before crashing on the moon?

____

6. How far will a skydiver have fallen before the parachute opens if the parachute opens 6 seconds after the diver leaves the aircraft?

____

IS YOUR ANSWER REASONABLE?
4.1054

NAME ____________________

SHARPEN YOUR SKILLS

Similar Figures

Find the missing measurements of these similar polygons.

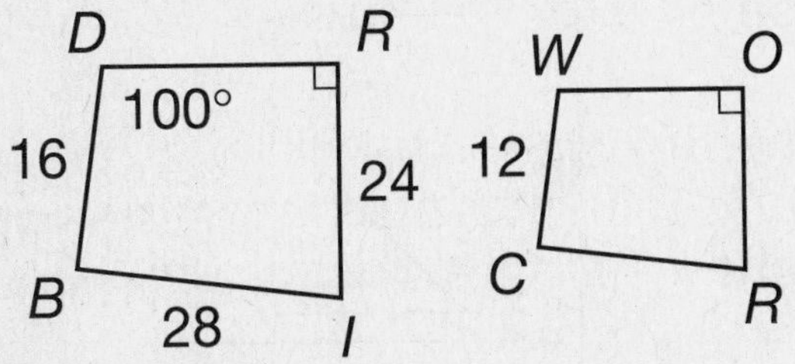

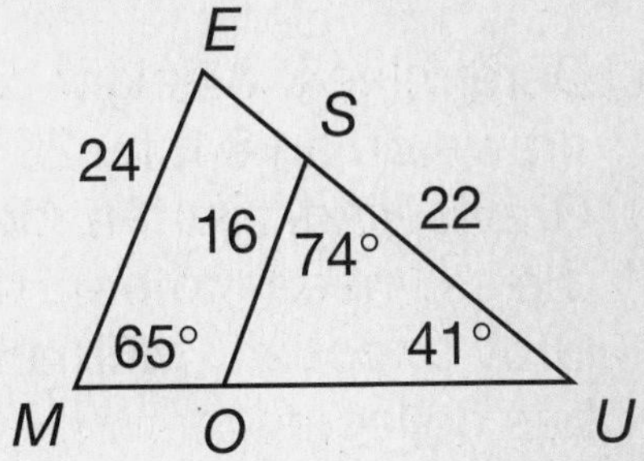

1. m ∠ *W* = ________

2. m ∠ *SOU* = ________

3. *CR* = ________

4. *EU* = ________

5. *RO* = ________

6. m ∠ *MEU* = ________

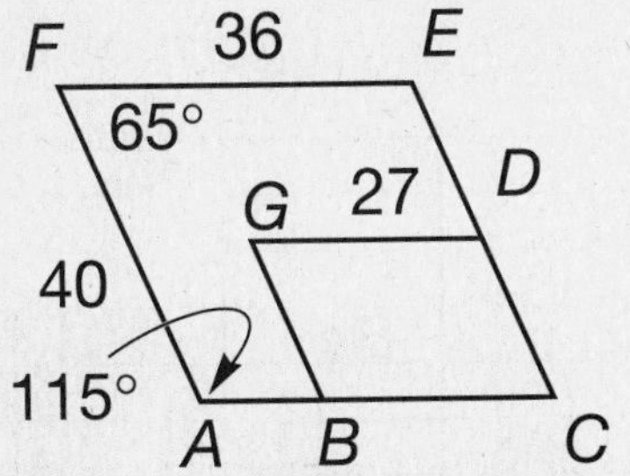

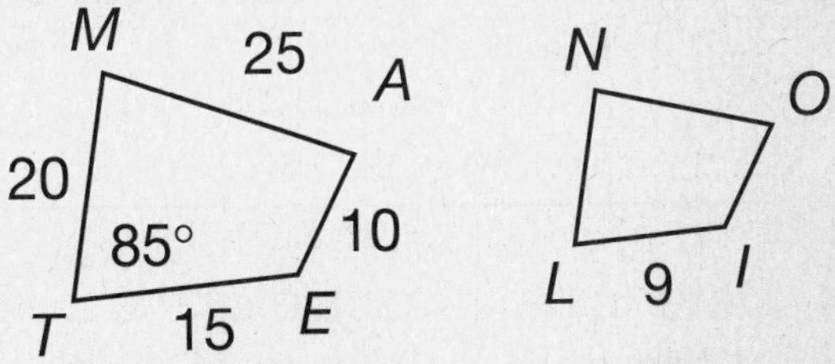

FEAC is a parallelogram.

7. m ∠ *GBC* = ________

8. *NL* = ________

9. m ∠ *BCD* = ________

10. *OI* = ________

11. *BG* = ________

12. *NO* = ________

13. *AB* = ________

14. m ∠ *L* = ________

15. Find the missing measurement of the three similar figures.

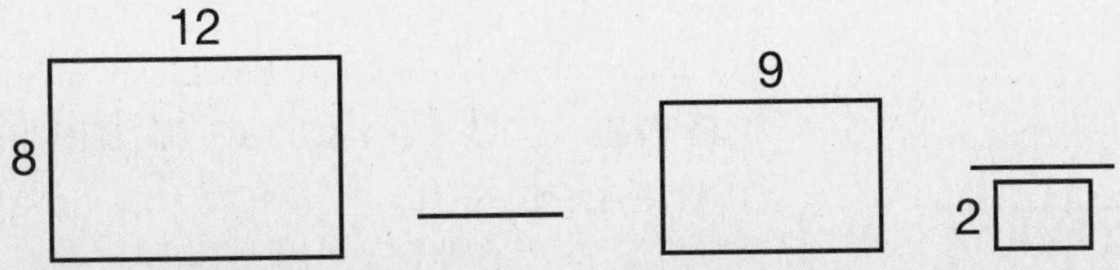

NAME ____________

SHARPEN YOUR SKILLS

Draw a Diagram

Solve the problem by using the grid method.

1. Determine the height of the sailboat to be drawn on an 8 ft by 20 ft wall in Mrs. Gray's kindergarten room. The height of the sail needs to be 3 ft in order for Mrs. Gray to cover it with a wallpaper scrap she has collected.

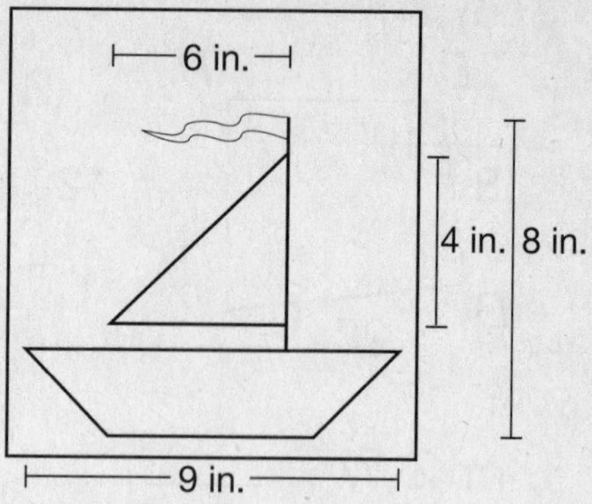

____

2. Determine the actual length of the sailboat in feet.

____

3. Determine the actual length of the base of the sail in feet.

____

4. Determine the scale of the bedroom shown at the right if the actual width of the bed is 60 inches.

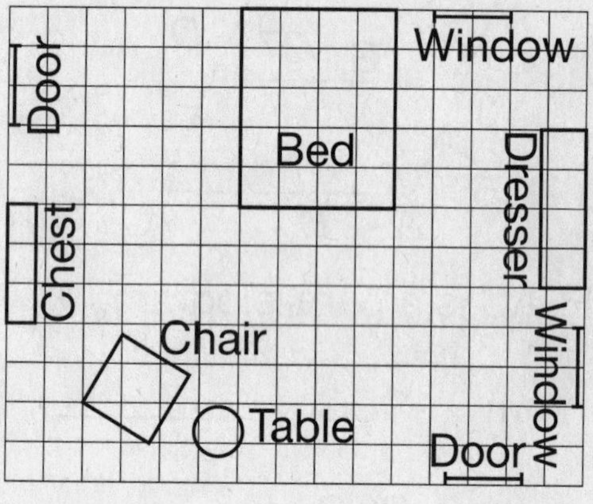

____

5. Determine the actual length of the bedroom in feet.

____

6. Determine the actual width of the bedroom in feet.

____

7. Determine the actual width of a window.

____

8. Draw on the diagram a 30 in. × 15 in. bookcase located against the wall and 15 inches to the left of the bed.

NAME ____________________

SHARPEN YOUR SKILLS

The Pythagorean Theorem

Find the missing side of the triangle. **Remember** that the hypotenuse is opposite the 90° angle.

1.

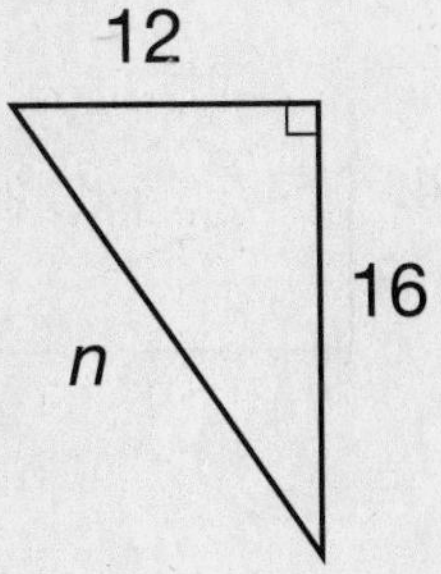

____

2.

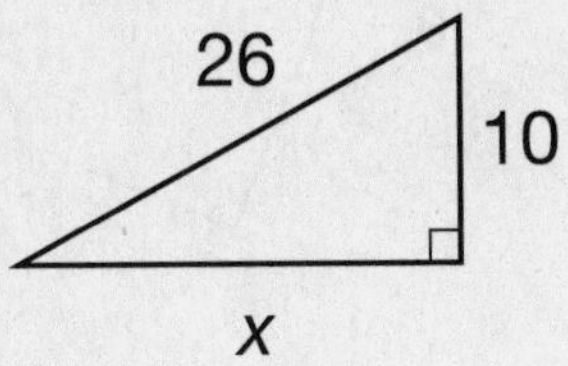

____

3.

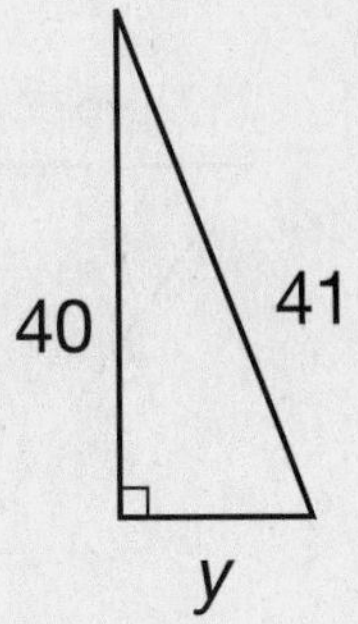

____

4.

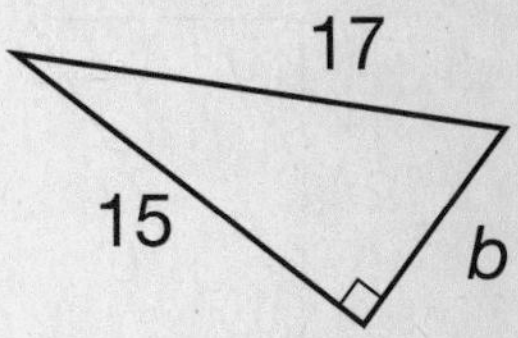

____

5.

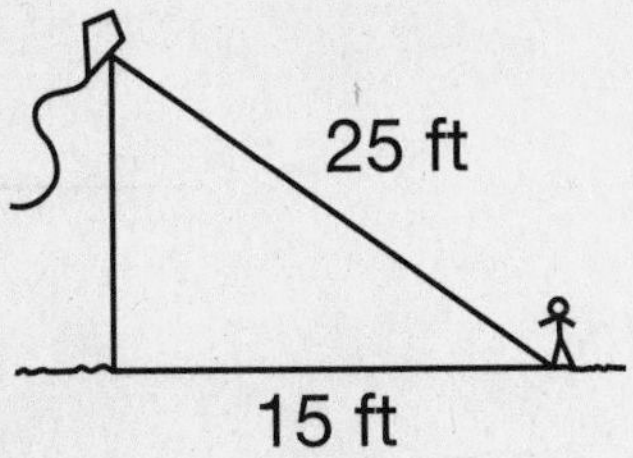

What is the height of the kite in the diagram?

____

6.

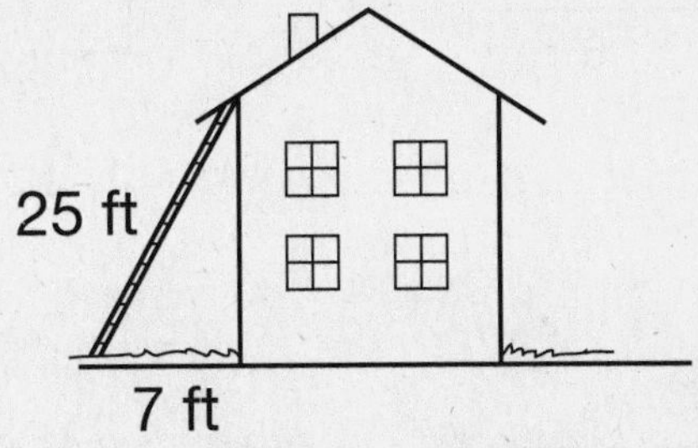

How far up the side of the house does the ladder reach?

____

7.

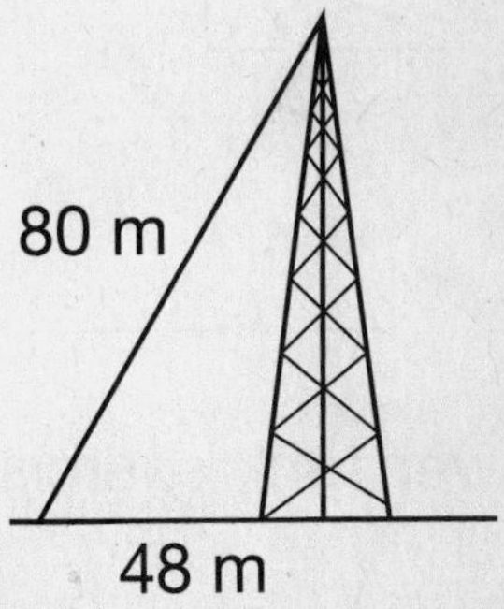

Find the height of the tower.

____

Solve the problem.

8. Juan left his campsite at Eagle Lake Park and hiked east for 6 miles. He then hiked due north for 8 miles. What is the shortest distance back to his campsite?

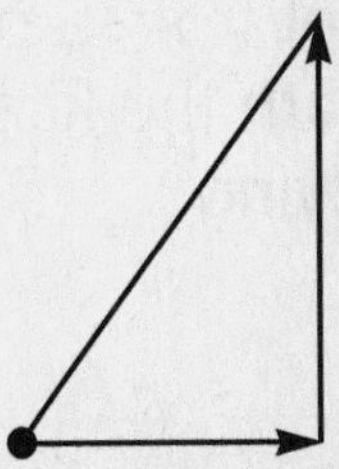

____

NAME

Using the Pythagorean Theorem

SHARPEN YOUR SKILLS

Use the Pythagorean theorem to find the missing measurements. Use a calculator, and round your answers to the nearest tenth when necessary.

1.
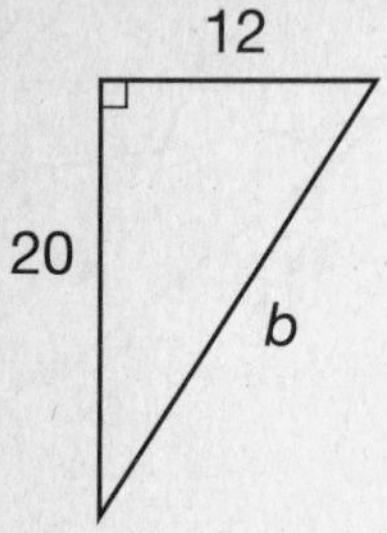

2.
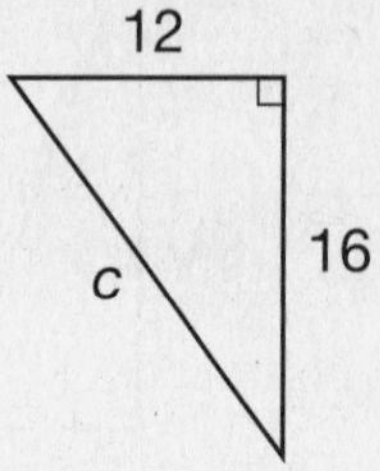

3.
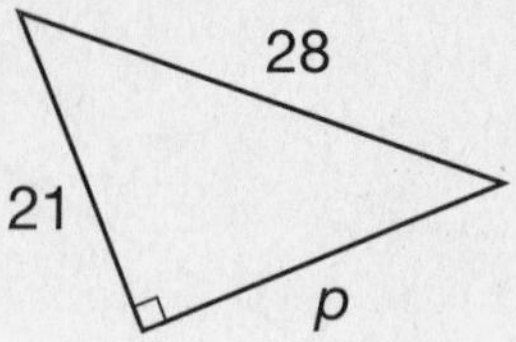

4.
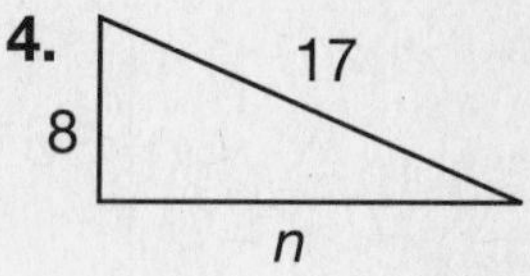

5.
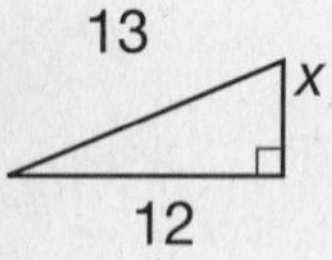

6.
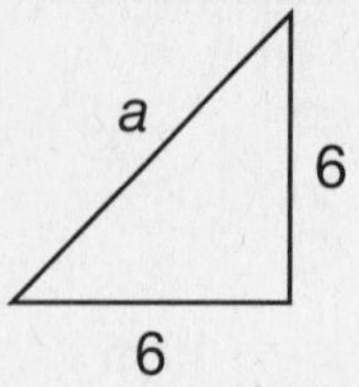

7.
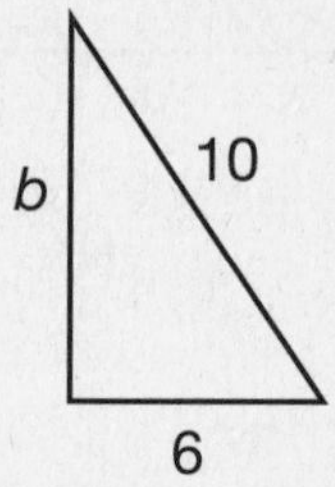

8.
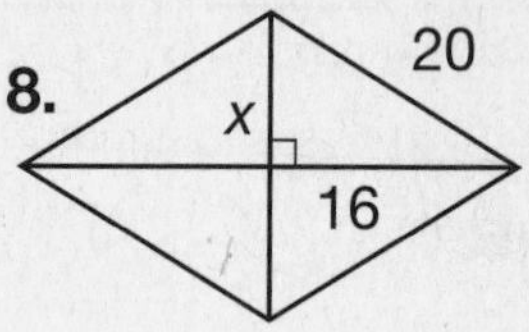

Answer each exercise.

9. The sides of a rectangle are 7 and 4. Find the length of the diagonal.

10. An isosceles triangle has a base of 40 and an altitude of 15. What is the length of a side of the triangle?

11. The kite string that Katie uses is 48 feet long. If she is standing 20 feet from a point directly beneath the kite, how high is the kite flying?

12. A 26-foot ladder just reaches a window that is 24 feet above the ground. How far is the bottom of the ladder from the base of the wall?

NAME

SHARPEN YOUR SKILLS

Pythagorean Triples

Use the Pythagorean Theorem and a calculator to verify whether these triples are Pythagorean triples.

1. 30, 40, 50 ______

2. 45, 60, 120 ______

3. 9, 16, 25 ______

4. 1.5, 2, 2.5 ______

5. $\frac{3}{4}$, 1, $1\frac{1}{4}$ ______

6. 10, 11, 15 ______

Mental Math Complete each table so that each Pythagorean triple is a member of the indicated right triangle family.

7.

8	15	17
24		
		85
	150	

8.

9	40	41
	120	
		164
90		

9.

0.5	1.2	1.3
1		
	6	
		7.8

Use Pythagorean triples to solve each problem.

10.

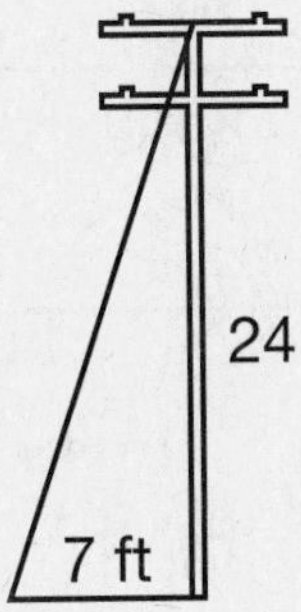

How long is the guide wire?

______

11.

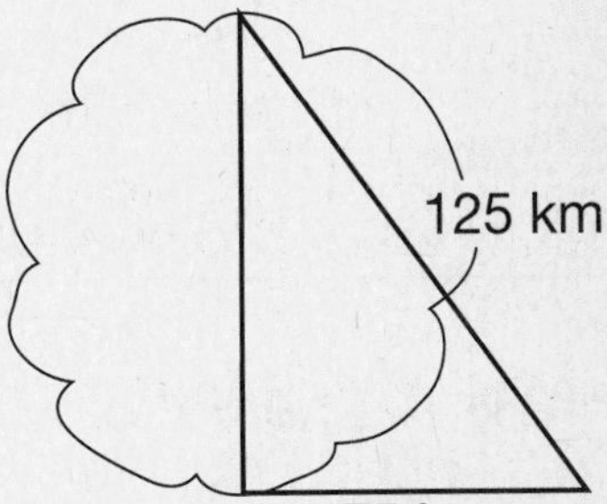

What is the distance across the lake?

______

NAME

SHARPEN YOUR SKILLS

30–60–90 Triples

Use a calculator to find the measurements for each figure. Round your answers to the nearest tenth.

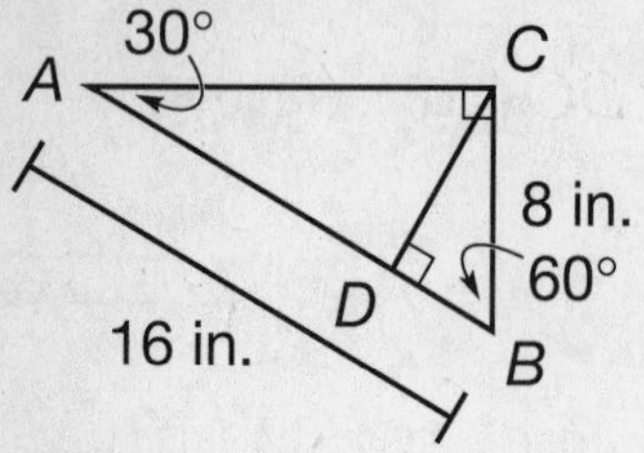

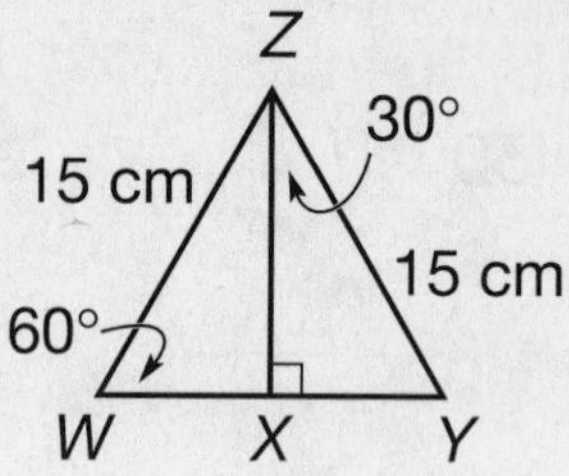

1. m∠ACD = ________
2. m∠BCD = ________
3. AB = ________
4. AC = ________
5. DB = ________
6. m∠WZX = ________
7. m∠XYZ = ________
8. WX = ________
9. XY = ________

Solve each problem.

10. The legs of a swing set form 60° angles with the ground and are 8 ft apart on each end. Find the height of the swing set.

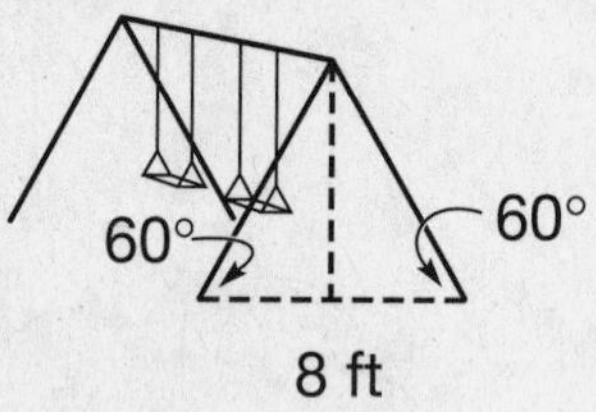

____

11. A ladder rests against a wall of a house at a 60° angle with the ground. The bottom of the ladder is 15 ft from the house. How long is the ladder?

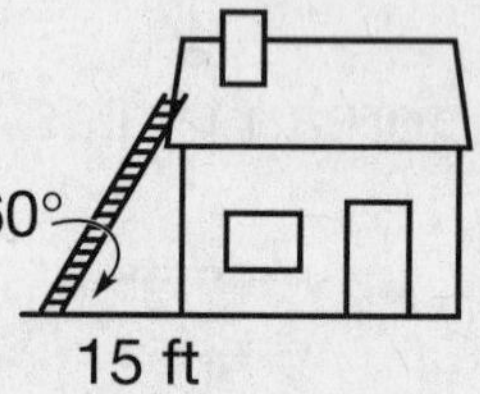

____

12. What is the height of △ABC?

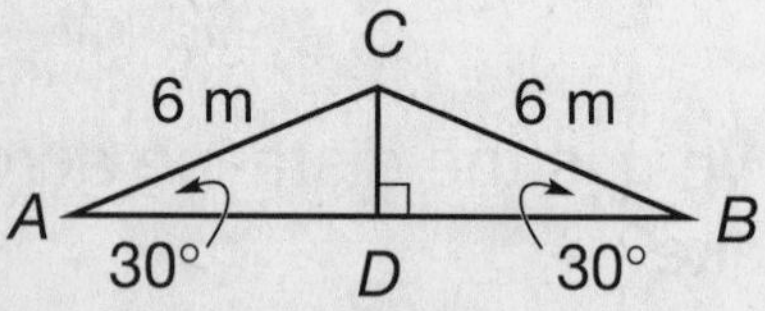

____

13. Mark travels 5 km east and then 12 km north. How far is he from his starting point?

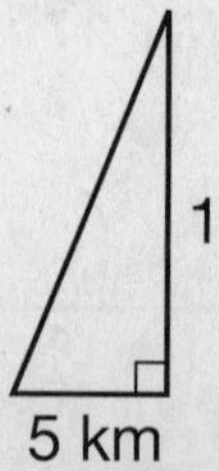

____

NAME

SHARPEN YOUR SKILLS

45–45–90 Triples

Use the figures to find the indicated measurement. Leave lengths in square root form.

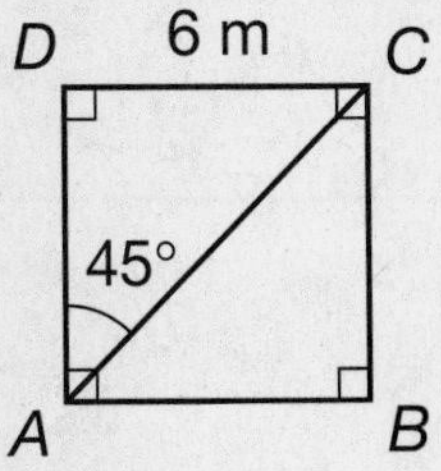

1. $m\angle CAB$ = ____________ **2.** $m\angle DCA$ = ____________

3. AD = ____________ **4.** AC = ____________

5. Area of $ABCD$ = ________

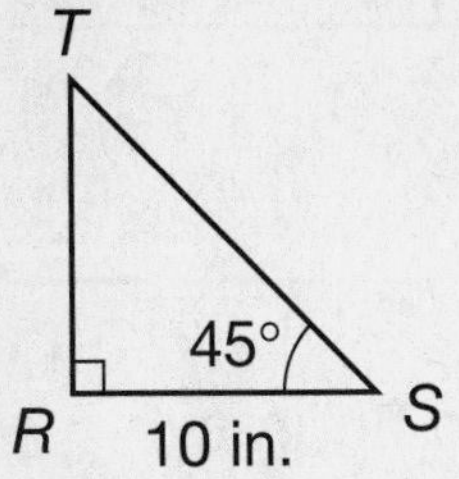

6. $m\angle RTS$ = ____________ **7.** RT = ____________

8. TS = ____________ **9.** Area of $\triangle RST$ = ________

Mixed Practice Use the figures to find the indicated measurements to the nearest tenth. Use 45–45–90 triples, 30–60–90 triples, or Pythagorean triples.

10.

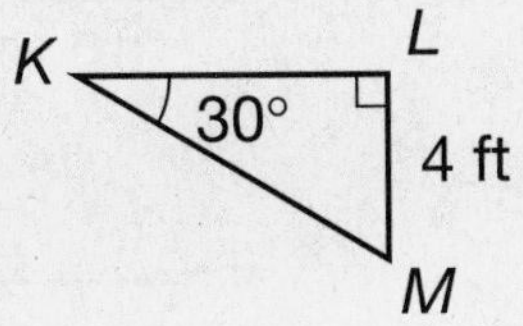

KM = ________

11.

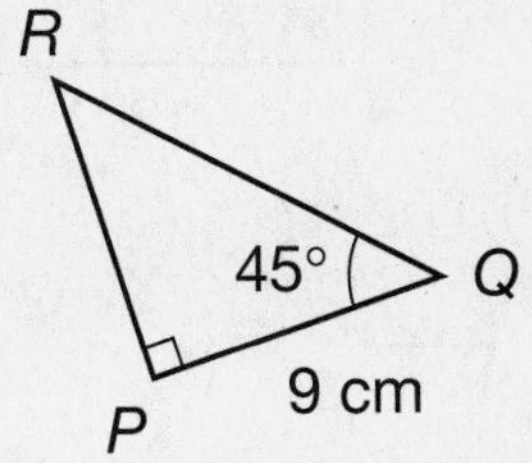

RQ = ________

12.

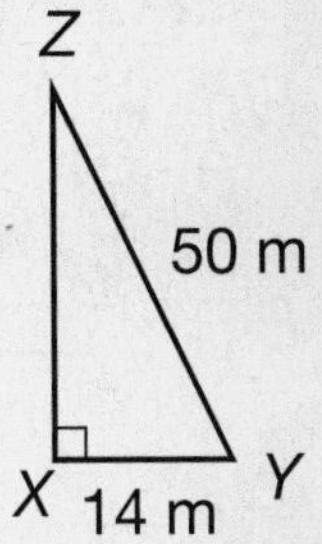

XZ = ________

Solve each problem. Round your answers to the nearest tenth if necessary.

13. Mrs. Browning is planning a flower garden in the shape of a square. She plans to construct a diagonal walkway through the flower garden. What will be the length of the walkway if the flower garden is 12 ft long?

____

14. If Mrs. Browning plans to make the walkway 2 feet wide, what will be the area of the walkway?

____

Use after pages 448–449.

NAME

SHARPEN YOUR SKILLS

Tangent Ratio

Write *always, sometimes,* or *never* to indicate whether the statement is always true, sometimes true, or never true.

1. The leg opposite an acute angle in a right triangle is longer than the leg adjacent to that angle. __________

2. The leg adjacent to an acute angle is longer than the hypotenuse of the triangle. __________

3. There is at least one acute angle in a right triangle. __________

Use the table on page 603 to determine each angle in the given figures.

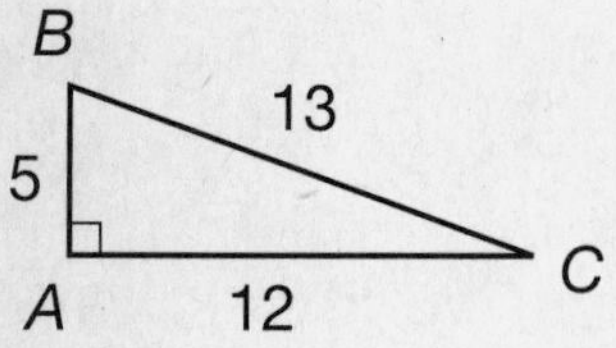

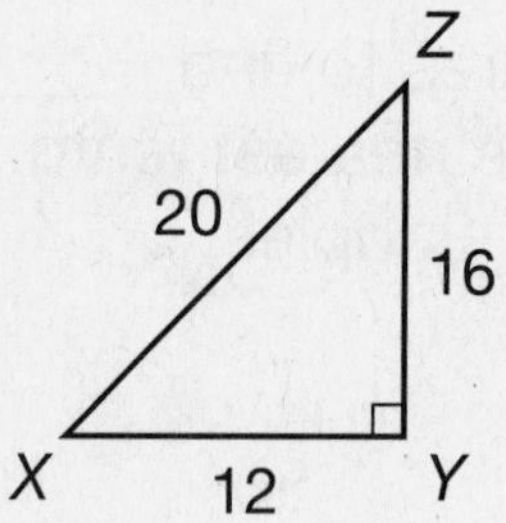

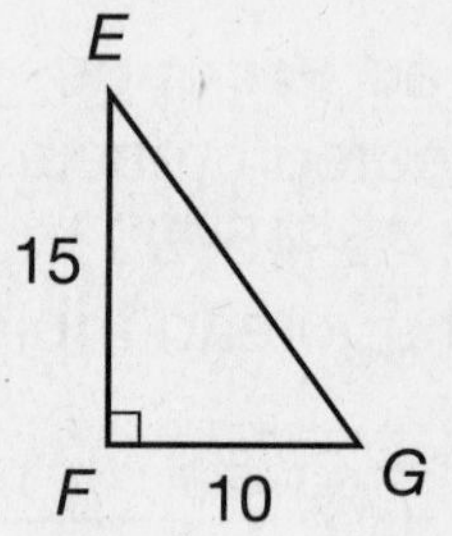

4. $\angle B$ = __________ **5.** $\angle C$ = __________ **6.** $\angle X$ = __________

7. $\angle Z$ = __________ **8.** $\angle E$ = __________ **9.** $\angle G$ = __________

Find the length of *X* to the nearest tenth for each triangle.

10.

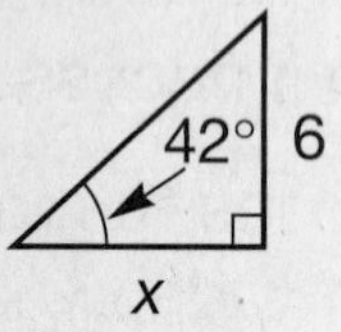

11.

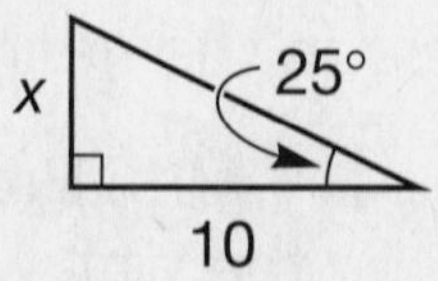

12.

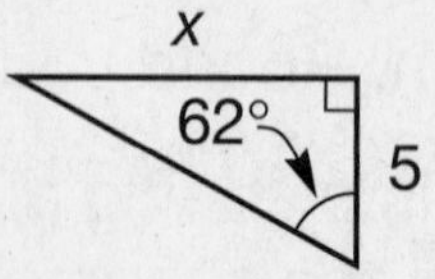

13.

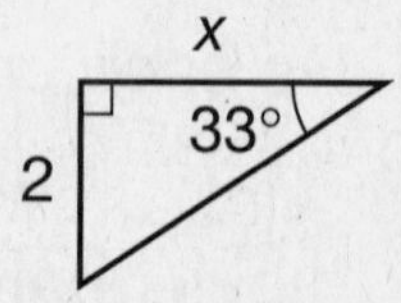

__________ __________ __________ __________

Use after pages 450–453.

NAME

SHARPEN YOUR SKILLS

Use Alternate Strategies

Solve each problem by using the Pythagorean Theorem, Pythagorean triples, or the tangent ratio. Tell which method you use. Round answers to the nearest whole number.

1.

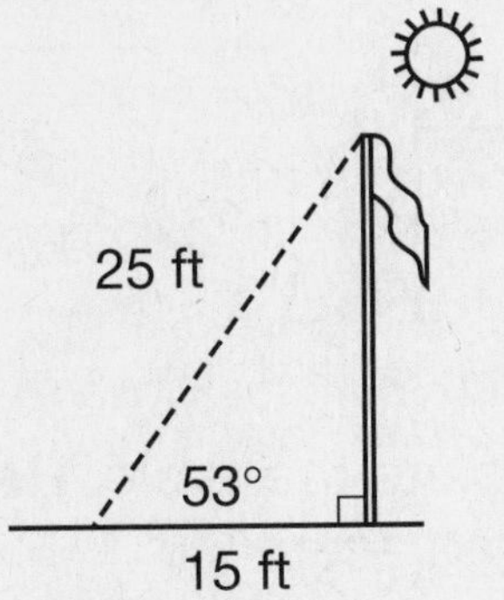

The diagram shows the shadow cast by a flagpole. What is the height of the flagpole?

______

2.

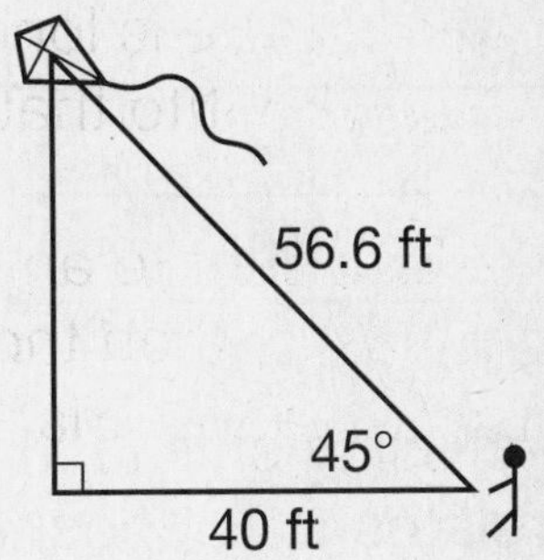

The diagram shows a kite flying. Find the height of the kite.

______

3.

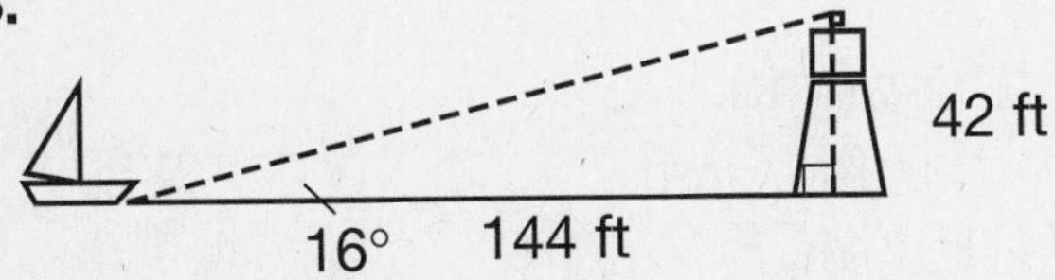

Find the distance from the sailboat to the top of the lighthouse.

______

4.

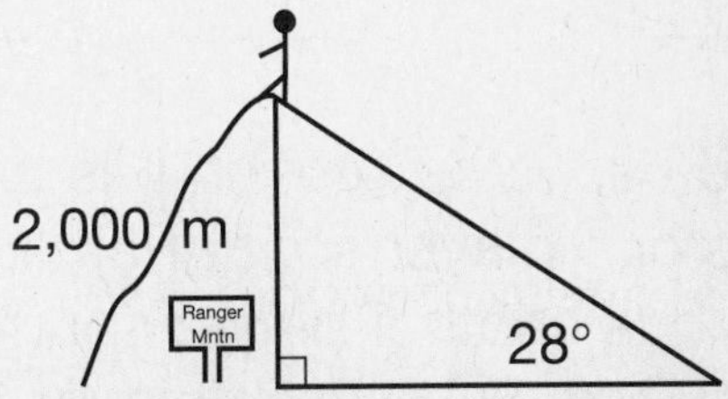

What is the length of the base of the ski slope at Ranger Mountain?

______

5. In Exercise 4, what is the length of the ski slope at Ranger Mountain?

______

6. Find the height of the tree trunk.

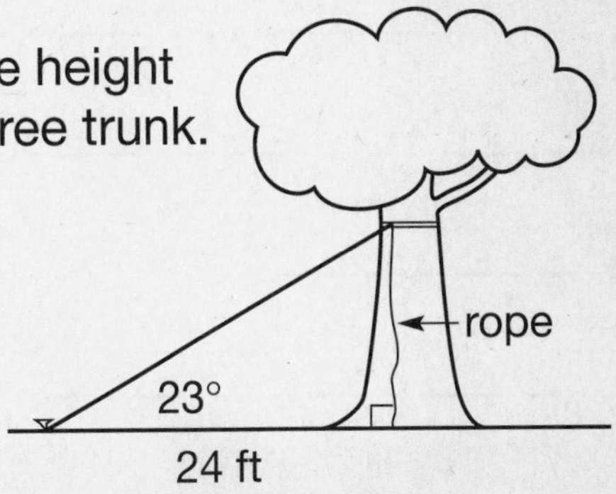

______

7. Find the length of the rope tied to the tree in Exercise 6.

______

NAME

SHARPEN YOUR SKILLS

Sine and Cosine Ratios

Complete the table using triangle *RST*. Record the ratio, the value, and the angle measure. Tell whether you use paper and pencil or calculator.

	sin	cos	tan	angle measure
∠*S*	**1.**	**2.**	**3.**	**4.**
∠*T*	**5.**	**6.**	**7.**	**8.**

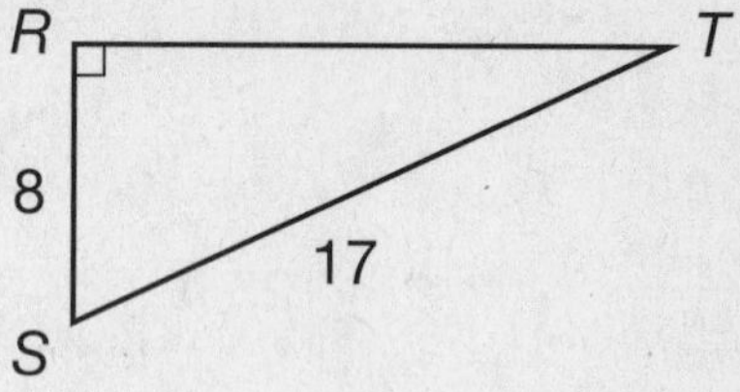

Find the missing side in triangle *ABC*. Then complete the table. **Remember** that sin relates to "opposite" and cos relates to "adjacent".

9. *BC* = ☐

	sin	cos	tan
∠*B*	**10.**	**11.**	**12.**
∠*C*	**13.**	**14.**	**15.**

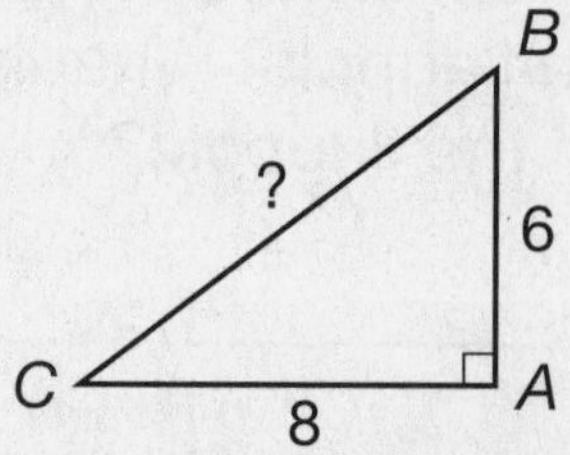

16. The basketball coach has his players run sprints. He has one player sprint Path *BEG* and then Path *GEB.* He has another player sprint Path *ADH,* Path *CF,* and Path *FC.* Which player runs the shorter distance? How do you know? Each box is a square.

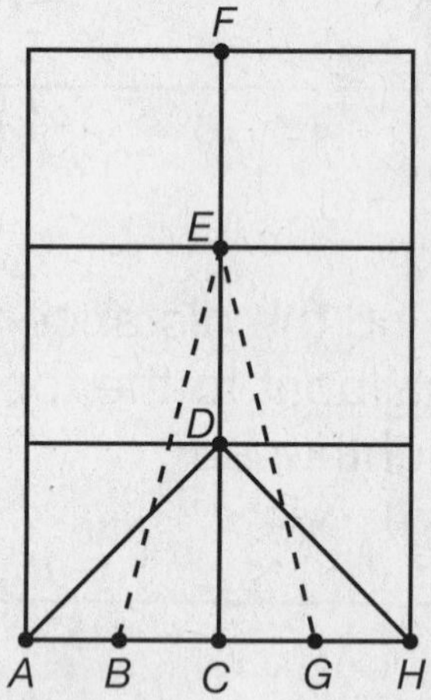

NAME

SHARPEN YOUR SKILLS

Organizing Data

For Exercises 1–4, tell whether you would use mental math, paper and pencil, or a calculator. Then use the following list of scores Nancy made on 20 daily exercises.

6, 8, 4, 8, 7, 5, 6, 9, 9, 10, 8, 7, 9, 10, 10, 8, 5, 4, 7, 9

1. Make a frequency table for the scores.

2. Find the mean of Nancy's daily scores.

____

3. Find the median of the data.

____

4. Find the mode of the data.

____

The table shows the number of farms in five states in the United States in 1989.

5. Calculate the mean number of farms in the five states.

____

6. Find the median number of farms.

____

States and numbers of Farms	
State	Number (in Thousands)
Iowa	103
Kentucky	96
Missouri	108
Tennessee	91
Texas	186

NAME

SHARPEN YOUR SKILLS

Stem-and-Leaf Plots

For Exercise 1, use the data to make a stem-and-leaf plot.

1. 134, 145, 155, 143, 138, 133, 147, 160, 152, 168, 132, 139, 141, 131

2. Use these sets of data to make a back-to- back stem-and-leaf plot.

1st Set: 41, 21, 34, 63, 63, 7, 11, 10, 12, 11, 12, 43, 49, 31, 40

2nd Set: 49, 41, 58, 63, 68, 85, 45, 63, 59, 24, 59, 55, 49, 39, 50

3. Find the range for each set of data in Exercise 2.

1st ________ 2nd ________

4. Find the median for each set.

1st ________ 2nd ________

The following stem-and-leaf plots are for the heights (in inches) of two groups of young people, a group of 5-year-olds and a group of high school students.

A.

0	
1	
2	
3	9
4	4 4 5 2 7 6 4 3 5 3 4 5
5	
6	
7	

B.

0	
1	
2	
3	
4	
5	8 9
6	1 2 6 8 8 5 7 6
7	0 1 2

5. Which plot most likely represents the 5-year-olds? Why?

____

____

____

____

NAME

SHARPEN YOUR SKILLS

Box Plots

Make a box plot for each set of data. **Remember** to represent outliers with an *.

1. 38, 41, 40, 58, 37, 29, 43

2. 161, 152, 167, 158, 163, 155

3. 78, 79, 71, 73, 80, 100

The table at the right shows Betty's grades in math for the first and second six-weeks.

First 6-weeks	Second 6-weeks
78	87
82	88
85	89
79	90
81	91
77	92
80	93

5. Arrange the data for each six weeks in increasing order.

1st ______________________

2nd ______________________

6. Find the median of each set of data.

1st ______ 2nd ______

7. Find the upper quartile for each set of data.

1st ______ 2nd ______

8. Find the lower quartile for each set of data.

1st ______ 2nd ______

9. Make a side-by-side box plot of the two sets of data on the line provided.

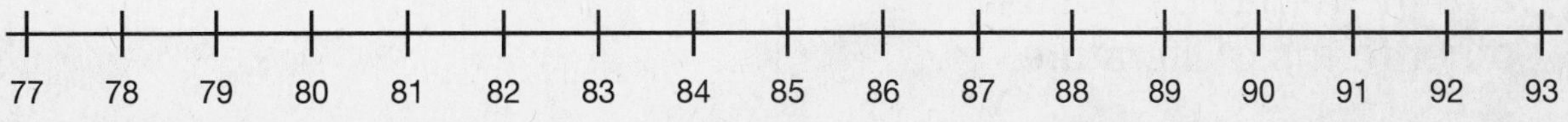

NAME

SHARPEN YOUR SKILLS

Using Graphs to Display Data

For each set of data in Exercises 1–2, make a bar graph and a circle graph.

1. Classifications of the members of the Spanish Club

sixth graders—14
seventh graders—32
eighth graders—43

2. How the membership dues of the Spanish Club were spent

Spanish video rentals—$30
Guest speaker fee—$25
Books about Spain for library—$48
End-of-school party—$89

3. Make an appropriate graph to display the following data: 300 members of the public library were surveyed about the kind of literature they preferred to read. 105 preferred novels, 95 preferred science fiction, 85 preferred mysteries, and the remainder preferred other forms of literature.

NAME

SHARPEN YOUR SKILLS

Bar Graphs and Histograms

The double-bar graph shows U.S. trade with Mexico over a four-year period.

1. About how many billions of dollars worth of goods did the U.S. export to Mexico in 1982?

____

2. About how many billions of dollars worth of goods did the U.S. import from Mexico in 1980?

____

3. About how much did U.S. exports to Mexico decrease from 1980 to 1983?

____

Look at the data in the histogram.

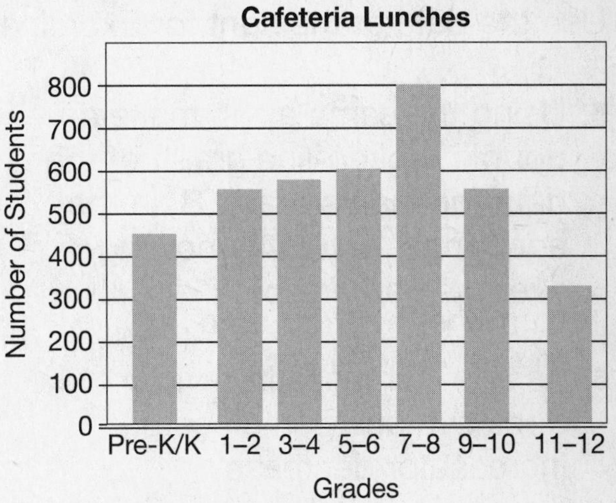

4. What range represents the greatest number of students buying lunch in the cafeteria?

____

5. About how many first and second grade students buy lunch in the school cafeteria?

____

NAME

SHARPEN YOUR SKILLS

Broken-Line Graphs

This graph shows the predicted rainfall and the actual rainfall in Ames County in 1989.

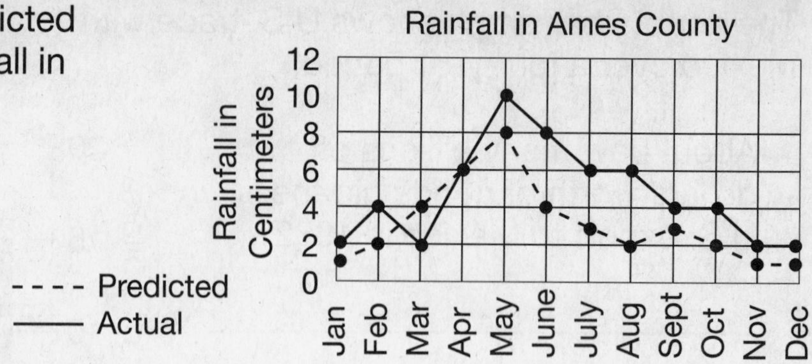

1. How much rain fell in Ames County in October? ____________

2. What was the predicted amount of rainfall for May? ____________

3. In which month was the actual rainfall the same as the predicted amount? ____________

4. For how many months was the actual rainfall more than the predicted amount? ____________

Use the data at the right for Exercises 5–6.

Age of Member	Average Game Scores	
	Team A	Team B
10	25	20
11	35	35
12	40	45
13	40	50
14	50	55

5. Using the same axes, make a double broken-line graph of the data for Teams A and B, in the age range 10 to 14, showing average game scores.

6. As age increases from 10 to 14, does average game score increase or decrease?

____

7. How can you tell? ____________

____

NAME

SHARPEN YOUR SKILLS

Use Data from a Graph

The graph shows the number of field goals attempted and made by a college team's football kickers.

Use the graph to answer the questions.

Field Goals Attempted and Made

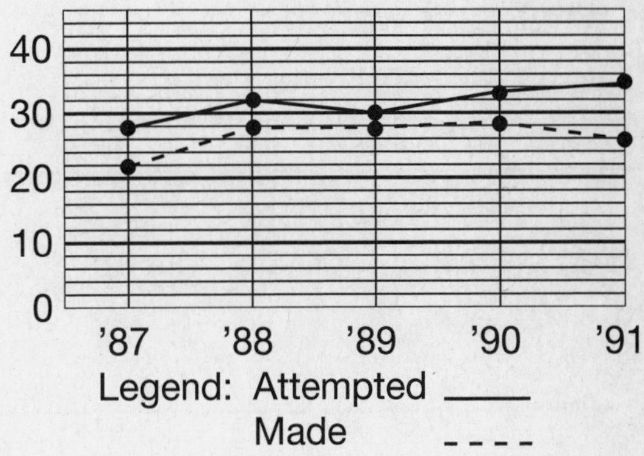

1. How many field goals were attempted in 1987?

____

2. How many field goals were completed in 1987?

____

3. Is the number of field goals made in 1991 greater or less than in 1987?

____

What is the ratio (expressed as a fraction and as a decimal) of field goals made to field goals attempted for each year?

4. 1987 ________________

5. 1988 ________________

6. 1989 ________________

7. 1990 ________________

8. 1991 ________________

NAME

SHARPEN YOUR SKILLS

Scattergrams

Use the scattergram to answer Exercises 1–4.

1. In what year was the record jump 27.5 feet?

____

2. What was the record jump in 1968?

____

3. In what years were the records above the line of best fit?

____

4. What would you expect the record jump in 1992 to be?

____

Olympic Records for Men's Long Jump, 1948–1988

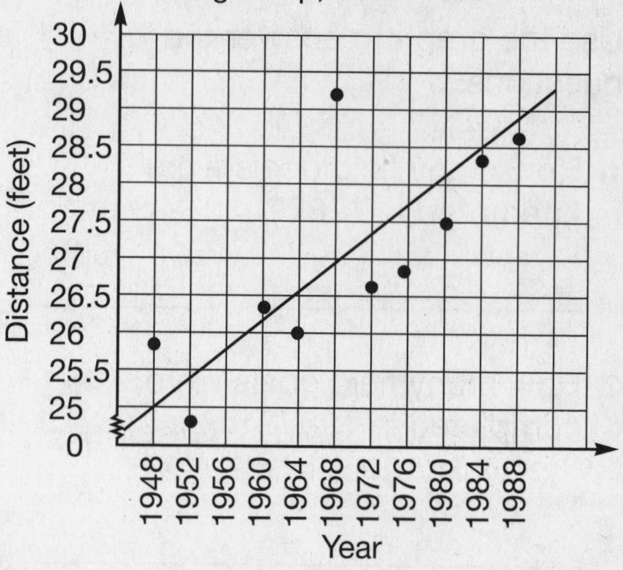

5. Make a scattergram using the data below. Then draw a line of best fit.

Olympic Records for Women's Long Jump

1952	20.4 feet
1956	20.8 feet
1960	20.9 feet
1964	22.2 feet
1968	22.4 feet
1972	22.3 feet
1976	22 feet
1980	23.2 feet
1984	22.8 feet
1988	24.3 feet

Olympic Records for Women's Long Jump, 1948–1980

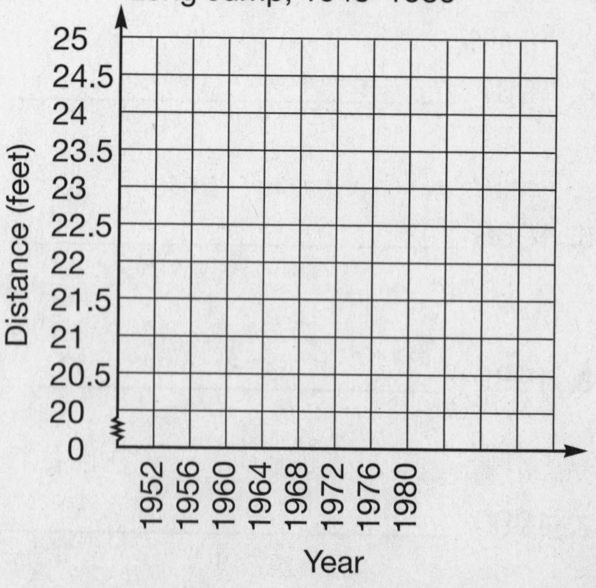

6. What would you expect the record jump in 1992 to be? ______________________________

NAME

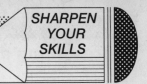

SHARPEN YOUR SKILLS

Sample Statistics

Describe the sample you would use to predict the sale of the following.

1. Health food ____________________

2. Acne cream ____________________

3. Dog shampoo ____________________

4. Grain harvester ____________________

5. Bowling balls ____________________

6. Snack crackers ____________________

Tell whether you would survey a sample closest to 0%, 5%, or 100%. Explain your thinking.

7. To find out how the students in Mr. Ferguson's class feel about the new bell schedule ____________________

8. To find out what number of citizens favor a particular political candidate

____

9. To find out how much exposure to the sun a human being can withstand

____

Mr. Milo conducted a survey to find the kinds of hamburgers preferred by the junior high students in the town where his cafe was located. He made hamburgers in three varieties: plain, with mushrooms added, and with onions added. Of the 216 surveyed, 54 students preferred the hamburgers with mushrooms, 145 preferred hamburgers with onions, and 17 preferred plain hamburgers.

10. Give the ratio of the number of students who preferred each type.

Mushrooms __________ Onions __________ Plain __________

11. Convert each ratio to a percent, rounding to the nearest whole number.

Mushrooms __________ Onions __________ Plain __________

NAME

SHARPEN YOUR SKILLS

Representing a Point of View

Tell how each graph could be changed to represent a different point of view.

1. Sleepyville City Debt

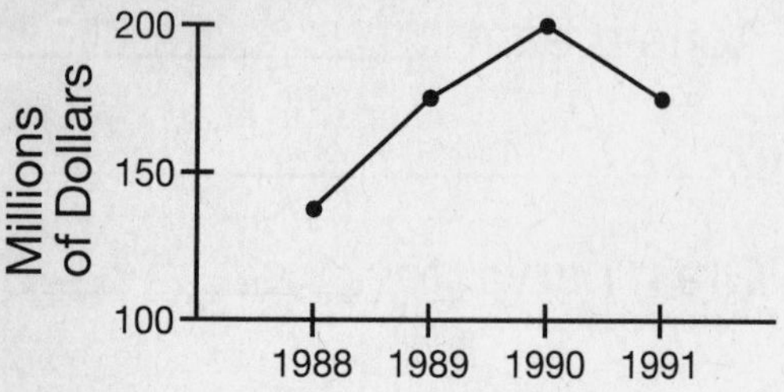

2. Average Land Values Sleepy County

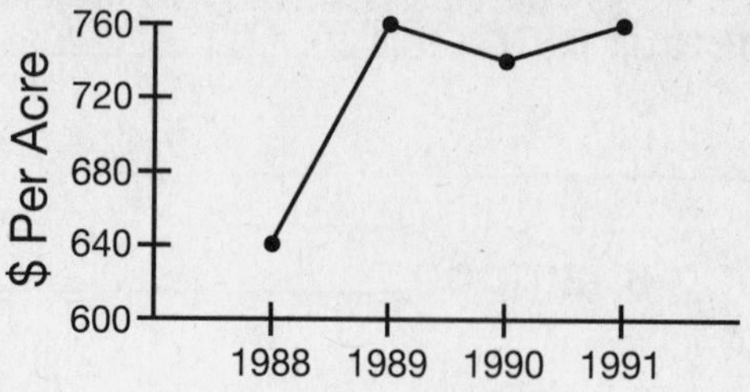

Look at these enrollment figures for Sleepyville Junior High School.

1988	1,610
1989	1,534
1990	1,372
1991	1,245

3. Make a broken-line graph showing that enrollment figures stayed about the same between 1988 and 1991.

4. Make a broken-line graph showing that enrollment figures dropped sharply between 1988 and 1991.

Use after pages 492–493.

NAME

SHARPEN YOUR SKILLS

Collecting Data

Fifty boys at a Florida junior high school and fifty boys at a Canadian junior high were asked, "In what sport do you most often participate?"

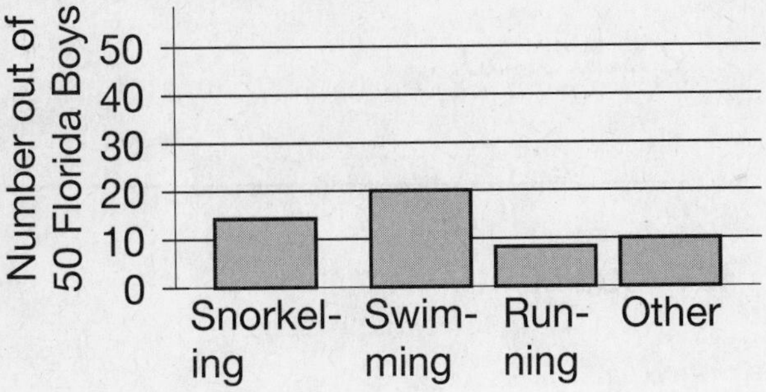

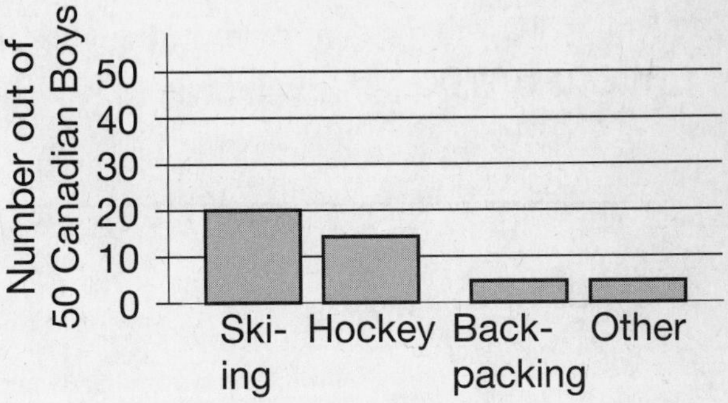

1. What factor is most likely to have influenced the boys' choices of participatory sport?

2. Is either survey a good representation of the preferred participatory sports of all North American eighth grade boys? Why?

Describe how you would collect data to find

3. how many students in your homeroom participate in a sport on a regular basis.

4. the kind of music most American eighth-graders prefer.

5. how many students in your school participate in a sport on a regular basis.

6. how many of the citizens of your city who voted for the current mayor are satisfied with his or her performance.

Use after pages 494–495.

NAME

SHARPEN YOUR SKILLS

Using Statistics to Make Estimates

Every year about 400 wild horses are captured, tagged, and released on the Island of Chincoteague. Then another sample is taken to estimate the total number of horses. Predict the total number of horses on Chincoteague if the samples show the average number of tagged horses is

1. 4 out of 100. __________

2. 2 out of 50. __________

3. 5 out of 8. __________

4. 1 out of 40. __________

5. 12 out of 50. __________

6. 9 out of 100. __________

7. 3 out of 400. __________

8. 6 out of 80. __________

Naturalists captured, tagged, and released 200 raccoons in Raccoon Forest. Predict the total number of raccoons in Raccoon Forest if the samples show that the average number of tagged raccoons is

9. 4 out of 50. __________

10. 5 out of 100. __________

11. 1 out of 40. __________

12. 7 out of 25. __________

13. 6 out of 100. __________

14. 3 out of 10. __________

NAME

SHARPEN YOUR SKILLS

Probability Experiments

A dietitian at a school cafeteria recorded the number of students buying various lunches during a two-week period.

Type of lunch	*Number of students*
Hot lunch	2,650
Sandwich only	1,100
Soup only	300
Soup and sandwich	950

Give the probability of each outcome.

1. P (a hot lunch) ______

2. P (a sandwich only) ______

3. P (soup only) ______

4. P (soup and sandwich) ______

5. P (soup only or sandwich only) ______

Estimation Select a story to read to a group of 8-year-old children. For Exercises 6-10, estimate the probability of each outcome: Like very much, Like, Neutral, Dislike or Strongly dislike.

6. P (Like very much) ______

7. P (Like) ______

8. P (Neutral) ______

9. P (Dislike) ______

10. P (Strongly dislike) ______

11. Draw a circle graph using the estimate from Exercises 6-10.

NAME

Use Data from a Table

SHARPEN YOUR SKILLS

Random Number Table

5	6	7	8	6	5	8	9	9	0	2	2	3	5	4	9	3	4	2	2
2	4	7	9	4	5	4	4	7	9	1	7	4	2	0	5	8	6	5	8
4	3	1	3	7	8	9	0	8	3	9	8	6	2	8	6	4	6	7	3
5	8	8	5	5	4	2	1	8	3	1	5	9	7	5	3	9	0	7	2
3	3	1	7	8	5	3	3	0	4	1	2	5	3	6	5	4	8	3	4
7	2	0	6	3	2	1	2	3	8	5	4	0	8	4	1	2	5	3	8
4	2	8	5	6	5	2	1	5	7	8	5	1	3	4	5	5	1	8	3
8	4	1	8	6	8	1	5	6	0	6	3	1	3	0	7	7	4	4	3
1	3	5	5	2	1	5	2	5	1	9	3	5	1	8	3	4	5	7	4
6	7	2	0	7	7	9	7	3	0	7	5	3	3	4	5	1	5	4	2

Predict the results of each experiment. Then use the random number table to simulate each experiment. Compare your predicted results with your experimental results.

1. While a machine was broken at a tennis ball factory, the probabilty of a ball being defective was $\frac{1}{10}$. How many tennis balls in a case of 60 were defective?

Prediction ____________________

Actual ____________________

2. Nathaniel has 5 pencils of different colors in a box. He selects one pencil at random and then replaces it. If one of the pencils is red, how many times out of 20 will he select the red pencil?

Prediction ____________________

Actual ____________________

3. If the probability of sighting a certain planet on an April evening is $\frac{3}{5}$, how many sightings is Janet able to get during the month? (Hint: Pick 6 numbers from 0 to 9 to represent planet sightings.)

Prediction ____________________

Actual ____________________

4. Alice has a box of 10 colors of beads in equal quantities. One of the 10 colors of beads is purple. If each of her 30 classmates selects a bead at random and then replaces it, how many times will a purple bead be chosen?

Prediction ____________________

Actual ____________________

NAME

SHARPEN YOUR SKILLS

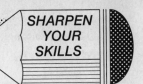

Fundamental Counting Principle

Tell whether you would use mental math, a calculator, or paper and pencil. Then find the total number of choices.

1. Stephanie has 6 scarves, 3 belts, and 2 hats.

____

2. Al's Cycle Shop has 5 bicycles, 1 basket, and 4 lights on sale.

____

3. Joan has 1 bookbag, 18 books, and 12 bookmarks.

____

4. Cullin's Pet Shop has 3 dogs, 5 collars, and 3 leashes for sale.

____

5. King Constantine had 4 crowns, 33 robes, and 24 rings.

____

For Exercises 6–8, use Rosie's Restaurant Menu.

Entrees	Beverages	Desserts
Beef plate	Milk	Fruit
Chicken plate	Mineral Water	Yogurt
Seafood plate	Bouillion	Ice milk
Chef's salad	Juice	

6. How many different meal choices (of 1 entree, 1 beverage, and 1 dessert) are possible?

____

7. If the beef and chicken plates are sold out, how many different meal choices are still possible?

____

8. If the beef plate sells out, and if a pork entree and another beverage are added to the menu, how many meal choices are possible?

____

9. A business executive must travel from Houston to New York to Copenhagen. Between Houston and New York she can travel by train, bus, car, or airplane. Between New York and Copenhagen she can travel only by airplane or ocean liner. In how many ways can her trip be made, including the return trip? ______________________

Use after pages 514–515.

NAME

SHARPEN YOUR SKILLS

Permutations

List the permutations. Then check your answer by calculating the number of permutations possible.

1. △○□

2. 

Tell whether you would use mental math, a calculator, or paper and pencil. Find the value of each of the following.

3. 9!

4. 11!

5. 2!

6. 4!

Solve each problem.

7. A gallery has 50 paintings in storage and space to hang 4 paintings along a hallway. In how many ways can 4 paintings be arranged to fill the display space?

8. How many different seating arrangements could a host consider at his table for 8 diners?

9. In how many different ways can a museum curator arrange 7 antique ornaments along a shelf?

10. A basket contains 11 buttons. In how many ways can 3 buttons be drawn (without replacement)?

NAME

SHARPEN YOUR SKILLS

Independent Events

Your teacher gave you a 2-question true-false quiz.

1. Complete the table showing all the possible patterns of true and false for the 2 questions.

	T	F
T		
F		

2. Refer to the table you made for Exercise 1. What is the probability that your pattern is the correct pattern if you guessed T, F?

____

3. Suppose your teacher gave you a 4-question true-false quiz. Make a table showing all the possible patterns of true and false for the 4 questions.

4. Refer to the table you made for Exercise 3. What is the probability that your pattern is the correct pattern if you guessed T, T, T, T?

____

You have 2 blue, 2 white, and 2 red socks in a drawer.

5. Complete the table showing all the possible patterns of socks you could pull out of the drawer if you pulled out only 2 socks.

	B	W	R
B			
W			
R			

6. Refer to the table you made for Exercise 5. What is the probability that the 2 socks you pulled out of the drawer is a pair of the same color?

____

NAME

SHARPEN YOUR SKILLS

Dependent Events

At her party, Shari had a grab bag. The chart shows how many bags contained each prize. What is the probability that

Prize	Number of bags
Key chain	6
Pen	5
Comb	4

1. the first two bags selected each had a key chain? ______

2. the first two bags selected each had a pen? ______

3. the first bag selected had a key chain and the second bag had a comb? ______

4. the first three bags selected each had a comb? ______

5. the first two bags selected each had a comb and the third had a pen? ______

Mixed Practice Tell whether Exercises 5-10 are independent events or dependent events: ______

Six cards are placed in a box. Three cards have a 2 on them, two cards have a 3 on them and one card has a 4 on it. If no replacement is permitted until both cards are picked, find each probability.

6. P (2, 2) ______ **7.** P (3, 4) ______ **8.** P (2, 4) ______

9. P (2, 3) ______ **10.** P (4, 4) ______ **11.** P (3, 3) ______

Solve.

12. Suppose there are 8 boys and 7 girls in the gym. If one student is chosen at random to run an errand, what is the probability that the student will be a girl?

______

NAME

Find a Pattern

SHARPEN YOUR SKILLS

Row		Sum
0	1	1
1	1 1	2
2	1 2 1	4
3	1 3 3 1	8
4	1 4 6 4 1	16
5	1 5 10 10 5 1	32
6	1 6 15 20 15 6 1	64

Pascal's Triangle

A family has 4 children, ages 11, 12, 13, and 14. Two of the children are girls and 2 are boys.

1. How many different patterns (birth orders of boys and girls) are possible?

2. Which row of Pascal's triangle helps you answer Exercise 1?

3. Write the numbers in the row you selected. Indicate which number tells the number of different patterns for 2 girls and 2 boys.

4. What do the other numbers in the row represent?

5. What are the possibilities (numbers of boys and girls) for a family of 7 children?

6. Edward and Diana play a set of 5 games of table tennis. What are the possible outcomes of the 5 games (numbers of wins and losses)?

NAME

SHARPEN YOUR SKILLS

Using Pascal's Triangle to Find Probability

Four light switches are equally likely to be on or off.

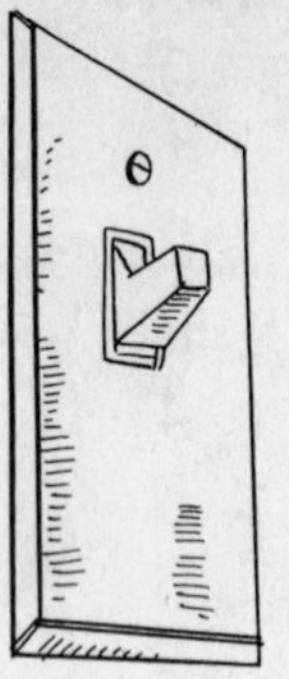

1. List all the possible arrangements of the light switches.

____

____

Find each probability for the 4 light switches, using Pascal's triangle where appropriate.

1 1
1 2 1
1 3 3 1
1 4 6 4 1
1 5 10 10 5 1
1 6 15 20 15 6 1
1 7 21 35 35 21 7 1

2. All on _____

3. 2 on, 2 off, in any order _____

4. In on-off-on-off order _____

Five light switches are equally likely to be on or off. Find each probability for the 5 light switches, using Pascal's triangle where appropriate.

5. All off _____

6. 4 on, 1 off, in any order _____

7. In this order: off-on-on-off-off

_____

Solve each problem.

8. In an experimental wind tunnel, 2 vents are equally likely to be open or closed. What is the probability that in the next experiment, 1 vent will be open and 1 closed?

_____

9. Best-selling books are equally likely to be checked out of the library or not. Of the 6 books Kari is interested in, what is the probability that all are in the library?

_____

NAME

Combinations

SHARPEN YOUR SKILLS

Use the words below for Exercises 1–3.

EVIL LIVE

1. Are these words different combinations of the letters L, I, V, and E? Explain.

2. Are these words different permutations of the letters L, I, V, and E?

3. How many 4-letter permutations of the letters L, I, V, and E are there? List them.

List and find the number of permutations and combinations. Then show how to calculate the number of permutations.

4. Only 2 of 3 interested students may represent the class in a calculator contest. How many possibilities are there?

5. Two hospital beds are available, but there are 4 patients waiting for beds. What are the possibilities?

NAME

SHARPEN YOUR SKILLS

Sets and Subsets

Write each set in roster notation.

1. $A = \{x \mid x$ is a composite number less than $10\}$ ____________

2. $B = \{x \mid x$ is a multiple of 3 less than $15\}$ ____________

3. $C = \{x \mid x$ is a positive number less than $8\}$ ____________

4. $D = \{x \mid x-1$ is a positive number less than $5\}$ ____________

Solve. **Remember** to include all members in the set. Use the sets *A*, *B*, *C*, *D* .

5. Write the set $A \cup B$ in roster notation. ____________

6. Write the set $A \cap B$ in roster notation. ____________

7. Write the set $B \cap C$ in roster notation. ____________

8. Write the set $B \cup C$ in roster notation. ____________

9. Write the set $A \cap C$ in roster notation. ____________

10. Write the set $A \cup C$ in roster notation. ____________

Critical Thinking Find each answer.

11. Find the total number of subsets of the set {1, 2, 3}. Remember to count the empty subset as one subset.

____

12. How many subsets does a set with 4 members have?

______

NAME

SHARPEN YOUR SKILLS

Venn Diagrams

Draw Venn diagrams to show the following. Label all diagrams.

Let A = {the first 5 letters in the English alphabet}
B = {the letters in the word *math*}
X = {the letters in the word *hat*}

1. $A \cup X$

2. $A \cap B$

3. $B \cup X$

Let $X = \{x \mid x$ is a positive number less than 5}
$Y = \{y \mid y$ is a positive number greater than 5 but less than 10}
$Z = \{z \mid z$ is a positive even number less than 13}

4. $X \cap Y$

5. $X \cap Z$

6. $Y \cup Z$

Mixed Practice Use your knowledge of sets and Venn diagrams to find each answer.

7. Use roster notation to show the intersection of all vowels in the words *onion* and *tomato*.

____

8. Use a Venn diagram to show the intersection of all vowels in the words *onion* and *tomato*.

NAME

SHARPEN YOUR SKILLS

Draw a Diagram

Use a Venn diagram to answer the questions.

In Mr. Jackson's eighth grade class, there are 24 students. Ten of the students are on the co-ed soccer team, 15 are in the art club, and 8 are on the soccer team and in the art club.

Mr. Jackson's class

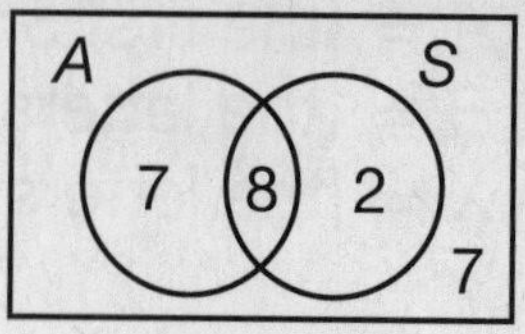

1. How many students play soccer but are not in the art club?

____

2. How many students are in the art club but do not play soccer?

____

3. How many students do neither activity?

____

In Nancy's classroom there are 20 students. On Monday morning, 13 people were wearing blue slacks, 6 people had on red shirts, and 10 people were wearing black shoes. Four people had on both blue slacks and red shirts and 7 had on both blue slacks and black shoes. No one wore all three—blue slacks, red shirt, and black shoes.

Nancy's class

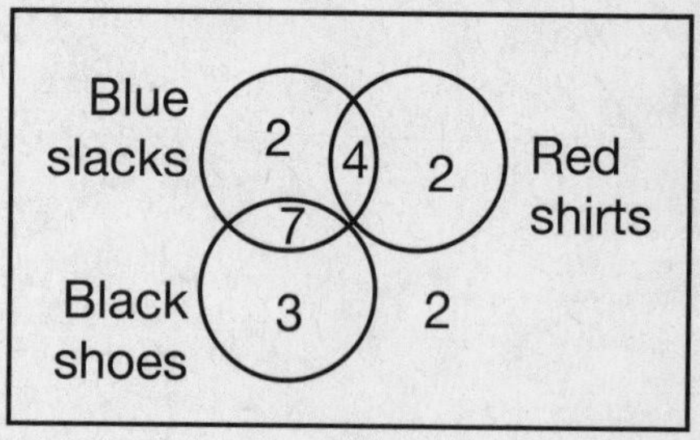

4. How many people were wearing black shoes but not blue slacks or red shirts?

____

5. How many people had on red shirts but not blue slacks or black shoes?

____

6. How many people were wearing neither blue pants, red shirts, nor black shoes?

____

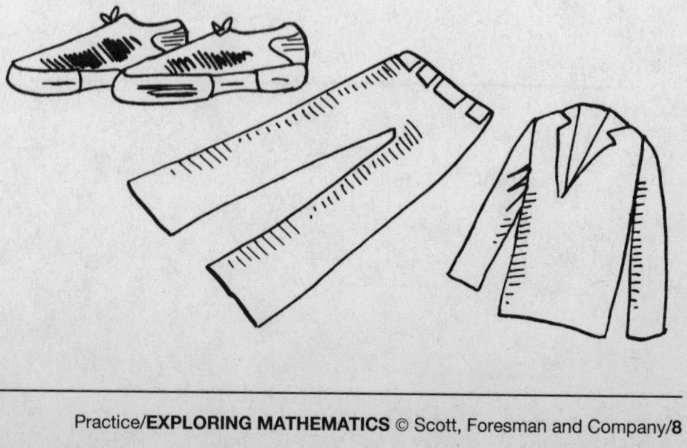

NAME

SHARPEN YOUR SKILLS

Compound Statements

Write the converse of each *if-then* statement.
Then decide whether the converse is *true* or *false*.

1. If 7 is a prime number, then 7 is an odd number.

2. If an animal is a dog, then the animal has 4 legs.

3. If a polygon has 4 sides, then the polygon is a square.

4. If today is Friday, then tomorrow is Saturday.

Solve each problem.

5. You choose one of the numbers 1–10 at random. What is the probability the number is less than 5 and a square number?

6. What is the probability that the number you chose in Exercise 5 is less than 5 or a square number?

7. The Jones brothers made the following statements:
Steven: "If the book is in the bookbag, then it is in the closet."
Brian: "If the book is not in the closet, then it is in the bookbag."
Alex: "If the book is not in the bookbag, then it is not in the closet."
Ken: "If the book is not in the closet, then it is not in the bookbag."
Steven told the truth. Who else must have told the truth?

8. The Smith children made the following statements:
Susie: "If the can is in the cabinet, then it is in the pantry."
Will: "If the can is not in the cabinet, then it is in the pantry."
Dan: "If the can is not in the pantry, then it is in the cabinet."
Bill: "If the can is not in the pantry, then it is not in the cabinet."
Dan told the truth. Who else must have told the truth?

Use after pages 552–555.

NAME

SHARPEN YOUR SKILLS

Work Backward

Solve each problem by working backward.

1. Jason bought a bag of baseball cards and shared them with his friends. He gave Juan $\frac{1}{2}$ of the cards plus 3 cards. He gave Susan $\frac{1}{4}$ of the cards left, plus three more cards. He then gave Ben $\frac{1}{3}$ of what was left. Jason then had only 10 baseball cards. How many did he begin with?

____

2. The Brown family rented a motor home for their vacation. They spent a total of $261.00 for the rental. The first day's rental was $36.00, the second day's rental was $39.00, and the rental for each successive day was $3.00 more than the previous day. For how many days did the Browns rent the motor home?

____

3. A painting contractor painted a warehouse. The painters used $\frac{1}{2}$ of the paint on the first day, and $\frac{1}{2}$ of the paint that was left on the second day. Then they used $\frac{3}{4}$ of the remaining paint on the third day and had 7 gallons of paint left. How many gallons of paint did they have to start with?

____

4. The 8th grade history class from Pizitz Middle School toured the State Capitol and the Archives Building at Montgomery, Alabama. Half the class went to the Archives Building where $\frac{1}{3}$ began in the Governor's office, 5 began touring in the chambers of the State Senate, and three began touring in the State Supreme Court office. How many 8th graders were on the tour?

____

NAME

SHARPEN YOUR SKILLS

Inductive and Deductive Reasoning

Tell whether you would use inductive or deductive reasoning to convince yourself that the statement is true or false.

1. If n is a composite number, then $n + 2$ is an even number.

2. The formula for finding the perimeter of a rectangle is $p = 2l + 2w$, where l is length and w is width.

3. The sum of any two even numbers is even.

4. If n is a whole number, then $n^2 + n$ is an even number.

Calculator Use a calculator to test each conjecture. If you think the conjecture is true, write *true*. If you think the conjecture is false, write *false* and find a counterexample to show it is false. **Remember** that n is a whole number.

5. $n^2 + n$ is an even number.

6. $n^2 + n + 17$ is a prime number.

7. $n^2 - n + 7$ is a prime number.

8. $n^2 - n + 4$ is a prime number.

Solve each problem. Tell whether you used deductive or inductive reasoning.

9. What is the next letter in the sequence?
a, e, i, m, q, …

10. John's father drives 120 miles at 60 miles per hour. How long did it take him to make the trip?

Use after pages 560–561.

NAME ____________

SHARPEN YOUR SKILLS

Use Logical Reasoning

At the annual Career Day assembly at East Middle School, speakers included Ms. Smith, Mr. Gomez, Ms. Tai, and Mr. Johnson, who were a teacher, a secretary, an engineer, and a truck driver, but not necessarily in that order. John knew that Ms. Smith was neither a teacher nor a secretary, that Ms. Tai was either a teacher or a truck driver, that the engineer was either Mr. Gomez or Mr. Johnson, and the secretary was not Mr. Johnson.

1. Set up a table that shows only the given information.

2. Decide who is the teacher, secretary, engineer and truck driver from the table in Exercise 1.

____

____

The manager, the accountant, the teller and the auditor at our local bank are Mr. Green, Mr. Brown, Mr. Gray, and Mr. Black, not necessarily in that order. Mr. Brown is taller than the auditor or the teller. The manager lunches alone. Mr. Gray plays bridge with Mr. Green. The tallest of the four plays basketball. Mr. Black lunches with the auditor and teller. Mr. Green is older than the auditor. Mr. Brown plays no sports.

3. Set up a table that shows only the given information.

4. Decide what job each man performs.

____

____

Use after pages 562–563.